California State Marine Fish

Garibaldi

A golden-orange fish approximately 14 inches in length, the garibaldi is most common in the shallow waters off the Southern California coast.

habitat range

thump *thump* *thump*

When disturbed, these fish emit a thumping sound that can be heard by divers.

HOUGHTON MIFFLIN

California
Science

HOUGHTON MIFFLIN   BOSTON

Program Authors

William Badders
Director of the Cleveland Mathematics and
Science Partnership
Cleveland Municipal School District, Cleveland, Ohio

Douglas Carnine, Ph.D.
Professor of Education
University of Oregon, Eugene, Oregon

James Feliciani
Supervisor of Instructional Media and Technology
Land O' Lakes, Florida

Bobby Jeanpierre, Ph.D.
Assistant Professor, Science Education
University of Central Florida, Orlando, Florida

Carolyn Sumners, Ph.D.
Director of Astronomy and Physical Sciences
Houston Museum of Natural Science, Houston, Texas

Catherine Valentino
Author-in-Residence
Houghton Mifflin, West Kingston, Rhode Island

Primary Grade Consultant

Kathleen B. Horstmeyer
Past President SEPA
Carefree, Arizona

Content Consultants
See Teacher's Edition for a complete list.

California Teacher Reviewers

Robert Aikman
Cunningham Elementary
Turlock, California

Christine Anderson
Rock Creek Elementary
Rocklin, California

Dan M. Anthony
Berry Elementary
San Diego, California

Patricia Babb
Cypress Elementary
Tulare, California

Ann Balfour
Lang Ranch Elementary
Thousand Oaks, California

Colleen Briner-Schmidt
Conejo Elementary
Thousand Oaks, California

Mary Brouse
Panama Buena Vista Union
School District
Bakersfield, California

Monica Carabay
Four Creeks Elementary
Visalia, California

Printed in the U.S.A.

ISBN-13: 978-0-618-68616-2
ISBN-10: 0-618-68616-9

Science Content Standards for California Public Schools reproduced by permission, California Department of Education, CDE Press, 1430 N Street, Suite 3207, Sacramento, CA 95814.

3 4 5 6 7 8 9-DW-15 14 13 12 11 10 09 08 07

California Teacher Reviewers (cont'd.)

Sheri Chu
Vineyard Elementary
Ontario, California

Teena Collins
Frank D. Parent Elementary
Inglewood, California

Gary Comstock
Cole Elementary
Clovis, California

Jenny Dickinson
Bijou Community School
South Lake Tahoe, California

Cheryl Dultz
Kingswood Elementary
Citrus Heights, California

Tom East
Mountain View Elementary
Fresno, California

Sharon Ferguson
Fort Washington Elementary
Fresno, California

Robbin Ferrell
Hawthorne Elementary
Ontario, California

Mike Freedman
Alta-Dutch Flat Elementary
Alta, California

Linda Gadis-Honaker
Banyan Elementary
Alta Loma, California

Lisa Gomez
Marshall James Elementary
Modesto, California

Lisa Green
Jordan Elementary
Orange, California

Carey Iannuzzo
Fitzgerald Elementary
Rialto, California

Teresa Lorentz
Banta Elementary
Tracy, California

Christine Luellig
Henderson Elementary
Barstow, California

Peggy MacArthur
Montevideo Elementary
San Ramon, California

Jeffrey McPherson
Parkview Elementary
Garden Grove, California

Susan Moore
Lang Ranch Elementary
Thousand Oaks, California

William Neddersen
Tustin Unified School District
Tustin, California

Josette Perrie
Plaza Vista School
Irvine, California

Lisa Pulliam
Alcott Elementary
Pomona, California

Jennifer Ramirez
Skyline North Elementary
Barstow, California

Nancy Scali
Arroyo Elementary
Ontario, California

Janet Sugimoto
Sunset Lane School
Fullerton, California

Laura Valencia
Kingsley Elementary
Montclair, California

Sally Van Wagner
Antelope Creek Elementary
Rocklin, California

Jenny Wade
Stockton Unified School District
Stockton, California

Judy Williams
Price Elementary
Anaheim, California

Karen Yamamoto
Westmore Oaks Elementary
West Sacramento, California

Contents

UNIT A
Life Cycles

Big Idea Plants and animals have predictable life cycles.

Reading in Science: Start with a Poem 2

Chapter 1 **Plant Life Cycles** 4

Vocabulary Preview 6

Lesson 1 How Do Plants Change During Their Life Cycles? . . 8

Extreme Science: What's the Big Stink? 16

Lesson 2 What Kind of a Plant Grows from a Seed? 18

Lesson 3 How Do Plants of the Same Kind Differ? 24

Focus On: Technology: Great Grapes 30

Lesson 4 How Do Plants React to Their Environment? 32

Links for Home and School 38

Careers in Science 39

Review and Practice 40

Chapter 2 **Animal Life Cycles** 42

Vocabulary Preview 44

Lesson 1 Which Baby Animals Look Like Their Parents? . . . 46

Lesson 2 Which Baby Animals Look Unlike Their Parents? . 52

Lesson 3 Where Do Animals Get Their Traits? 58

Extreme Science: Check Out These Chickens 64

Lesson 4 How Do Animals of the Same Kind Differ? 66

Focus On: Technology: Spin a Yarn 72

Links for Home and School 74

People in Science 75

Review and Practice 76

Scarlet Tanagers

Unit Review and Practice 78
Unit Wrap-Up 80

Activities

California Field Trip: Sequoia National Park . . Tab A

Directed Inquiry

Fruits and Seeds 9
Plant Seeds 19
Compare Pea Pods 25
Sprouting Seeds 33
Compare Life Cycles 47
Triops Stages 53
Train Goldfish 59
Measure Handspans 67

Express Lab

Order a Plant Life Cycle 11
Compare Young Plants to Their Parents 21
Compare Leaf Size 27
Compare Temperature 35
Match Animals 49
Measure How a Frog Changes 55
Observe a Learned Behavior 61
Compare Two Individuals 69

Jeffrey pine tree

Contents

UNIT B

Earth's Resources

Big Idea Earth is made of materials that have distinct properties and provide resources for human activities.

Reading in Science: Start with a Song	82
Chapter 3 **Rocks, Soils, and Fossils**	84
Vocabulary Preview	86
Lesson 1 What Makes Up Rocks?	88
Lesson 2 How Do Rocks Change?	96
Lesson 3 What Makes Up Soil?	102
Extreme Science: Mighty Mite	110
Lesson 4 What Clues Do Fossils Give?	112
Focus On: History of Science: Fossils of Saber-Toothed Cats	120
Links for Home and School	122
Careers in Science	123
Review and Practice	124

Chapter 4 **Using Resources**	126
Vocabulary Preview	128
Lesson 1 How Do People Use Rocks?	130
Focus On: Readers' Theater: Rock Stars	136
Lesson 2 How Do People Use Water?	140
Lesson 3 How Do People Use Soil and Plants?	146
Lesson 4 How Can People Save Resources?	154
Extreme Science: Trash Bird	160
Links for Home and School	162
People in Science	163
Review and Practice	164

Unit Review and Practice 166

Unit Wrap-Up 168

Activities

California Field Trip: Red Rock Canyon . . . . Tab B

Directed Inquiry

Compare Rocks. 89

Changing Rocks 97

Compare Soils. 103

Compare Fossils 113

Look for Rocks 131

Water Use. 141

Water in Soil. 147

Wasted Water. 155

Express Lab

Group Rocks 91

Observe How Rocks Change 98

Compare Soils. 106

Group Fossils. 117

Identify Rock Uses 132

Categorize Water Uses 143

Classify Soil 149

Model Water Waste. 156

Red Rock Canyon

Contents

UNIT C
Motion and Forces

Big Idea The motion of objects can be observed and measured.

Reading in Science: Start with a Poem 170

Chapter 5 **Objects in Motion** 172

Vocabulary Preview 174

Lesson 1 How Can You Describe an Object's Position? 176

Focus On: History of Science:
Measuring Tools Then and Now 182

Lesson 2 How Can You Describe an Object's Motion? 184

Extreme Science: Fast, Faster, Fastest! 192

Links for Home and School 194

Careers in Science 195

Review and Practice 196

Chapter 6 **Forces** 198

Vocabulary Preview 200

Lesson 1 What Do Forces Do? 202

Lesson 2 How Can You Change an Object's Direction? . . . 210

Focus On: Readers' Theater:
Motion at the California Speedway 216

Lesson 3 What Do Tools and Machines Do? 220

Extreme Science: Mega Mover 226

Lesson 4 What Makes Things Fall? 228

Links for Home and School 234

People in Science 235

Review and Practice 236

Unit Review and Practice 238

Unit Wrap-Up 240

Activities

California Field Trip: Spirit of Sacramento . . . . Tab C

Directed Inquiry

Locate an Object 177

Objects in Motion 185

Change Motion 203

Change Direction 211

Tools Push and Pull 221

Falling Objects 229

Express Lab

Describe an Object's Location 179

Observe a Ball's Motion. 187

Measure Motion. 207

Change an Object's Direction 212

Make a Machine. 223

Experiment with Gravity 230

San Francisco
cable car

Contents

UNIT D
Magnets and Sound

Big Idea The motion of objects can be observed and measured.

Reading in Science: Start with a Song. 242

Chapter 7 **Magnets** 244

Vocabulary Preview 246

Lesson 1 What Are Magnets? 248

Focus On: Technology: Maglev Trains 254

Lesson 2 What Is a Magnetic Field? 256

Lesson 3 How Strong Is a Magnet's Force? 260

Extreme Science: Magnet Power! 266

Links for Home and School 268

People in Science 269

Review and Practice 270

Chapter 8 **Making Sound** 272

Vocabulary Preview 274

Lesson 1 How Is Sound Made? 276

Focus On: Literature: *Wind Song;*
My House's Night Song 282

Lesson 2 What Is Pitch? 284

Lesson 3 What Is a Sound's Volume? 290

Extreme Science: A Whale of a Sound 296

Links for Home and School 298

Careers in Science 299

Review and Practice 300

Unit Review and Practice 302
Unit Wrap-Up 304

Activities

California Field Trip: Mariachi Festival . . . . . . Tab D

Directed Inquiry
Test Magnets 249
Filing Patterns 257
Observe Force 261
Making Sound 277
High or Low 285
Loud or Soft 291

Express Lab
Observe Magnets 251
Observe a Magnetic Field 258
Move Objects with Magnets 263
Observe Sound 279
Compare Sounds 287
Change Volume 293

The Rose Parade

Using Your Book

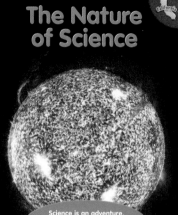

The Nature of Science

Science is an adventure. People all over the world do science. You can do science, too. You probably already do.

The Nature of Science

In the front of your book you will learn about how people explore science.

Every unit in your book has two or more chapters.

PHYSICAL **C** SCIENCE

Motion and Forces

Reading in Science 170

Chapter 5
Objects in Motion 172

Independent Books
• Objects in Motion
• Hide and Seek
• Going to the Races

Chapter 6
Forces 198

Independent Books
• Forces
• Moving Day
• Push or Pull

Big Idea!
Standard Set 1,
Physical Sciences

The motion of objects can be observed and measured.

Motion on a playground

169

You can read these on your own.

Big Idea! tells you the part of your **California Science Standards** that connects the ideas of each lesson.

Lesson Preview gives information and asks questions about each lesson.

Chapter **5**

Objects in Motion

San Francisco cable car

172

Lesson Preview

LESSON 1
The ball is next to the car. What other position words can you use to describe the location of the ball?

LESSON 2
These boys will run a race. As they race, how will you know who is faster?

My Journal
Write or draw in your journal to answer the questions above. 173

My Journal tells you to write or draw answers to the questions.

Vocabulary Preview

Introduces important science terms, with pictures, and vocabulary skills.

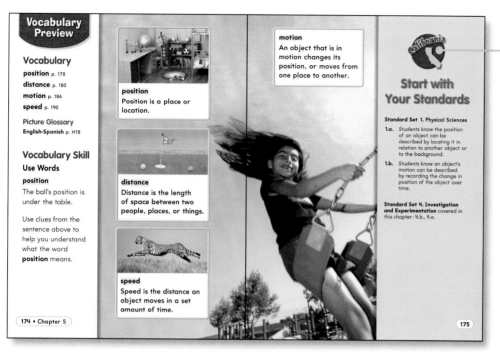

California Science Standards are identified for each chapter.

Every lesson in your book has two parts.
Part 1: Directed Inquiry

Building Background gives you science facts needed for the lessons.

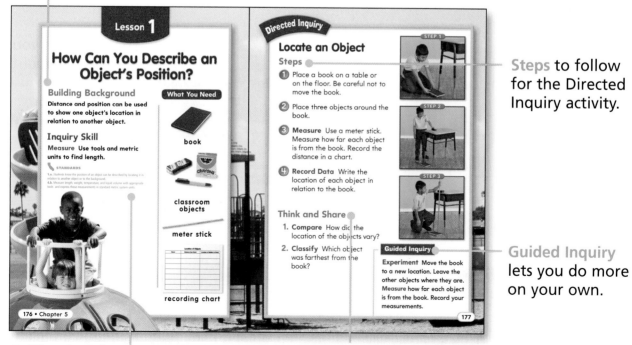

Steps to follow for the Directed Inquiry activity.

Guided Inquiry lets you do more on your own.

California Science Standards appear in blue throughout each lesson.

Think and Share lets you check what you have learned.

Part 2: Learn by Reading

Vocabulary lists the new science words you will learn. In the text, dark words with yellow around them are new words.

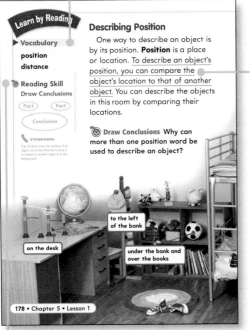

Learn by Reading

▶ Vocabulary

position
distance

⊚ Reading Skill
Draw Conclusions

Fact   Fact

Conclusion

STANDARDS
1.a. Students know the position of an object can be described by locating it in relation to another object or to the background.

Describing Position

One way to describe an object is by its position. **Position** is a place or location. To describe an object's position, you can compare the object's location to that of another object. You can describe the objects in this room by comparing their locations.

⊚ **Draw Conclusions** Why can more than one position word be used to describe an object?

Main Idea is underlined to show you what is important.

to the left of the bank

on the desk

under the bank and over the books

178 • Chapter 5 • Lesson 1

Reading Skill helps you understand the text.

Lesson Wrap-Up

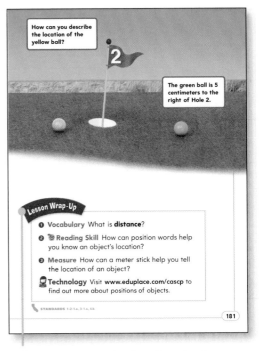

How can you describe the location of the yellow ball?

The green ball is 5 centimeters to the right of Hole 2.

Lesson Wrap-Up

❶ **Vocabulary** What is **distance**?

❷ ⊚ **Reading Skill** How can position words help you know an object's location?

❸ **Measure** How can a meter stick help you tell the location of an object?

💻 **Technology** Visit www.eduplace.com/cascp to find out more about positions of objects.

STANDARDS 1-2 1.a, 1 1.a, 4.b

181

After you read, check what you have learned.

Focus On

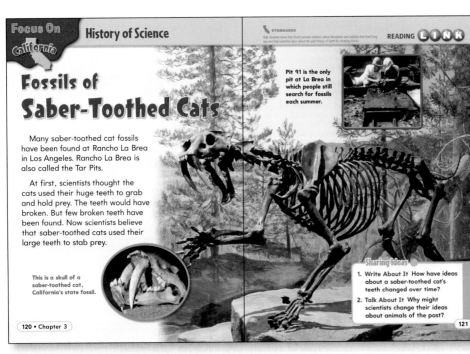

Focus On **History of Science**

Fossils of Saber-Toothed Cats

Many saber-toothed cat fossils have been found at Rancho La Brea in Los Angeles. Rancho La Brea is also called the Tar Pits.

At first, scientists thought the cats used their huge teeth to grab and hold prey. The teeth would have broken. But few broken teeth have been found. Now scientists believe that saber-toothed cats used their large teeth to stab prey.

This is a skull of a saber-toothed cat, California's state fossil.

120 • Chapter 3

STANDARDS
3-d. Students know that fossils provide evidence about the plants and animals that lived long ago and that scientists learn about the past history of Earth by studying fossils.

READING **LINK**

Pit 91 is the only pit at La Brea in which people still search for fossils each summer.

Sharing Ideas

1. **Write About It** How have ideas about a saber-toothed cat's teeth changed over time?

2. **Talk About It** Why might scientists change their ideas about animals of the past?

121

Focus On lets you learn more about an important topic. Look for History of Science, Technology, Literature, Readers' Theater– and more.

Sharing Ideas has you check your understanding and write and talk about what you have learned.

Extreme Science

Compares and contrasts interesting science information.

My Journal provides a chance to write your ideas about the Extreme Science lessons.

Links and Careers/People in Science

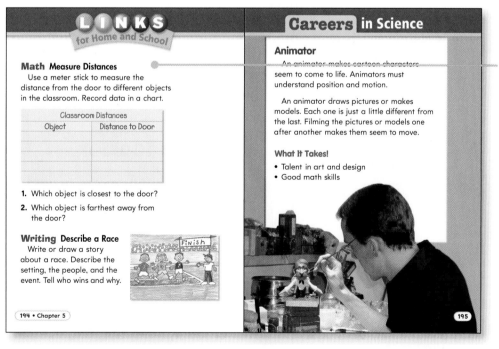

You can do these at school or at home.

Links connects science to other subject areas.

Careers/People in Science tells you about the work of a real scientist.

Review and Unit Practice

These reviews help you to know you are on track with learning California science standards.

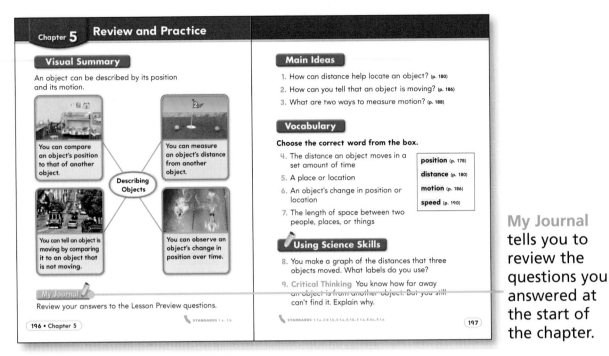

Chapter 5 Review and Practice

Visual Summary

An object can be described by its position and its motion.

You can compare an object's position to that of another object.

You can measure an object's distance from another object.

Describing Objects

You can tell an object is moving by comparing it to an object that is not moving.

You can observe an object's change in position over time.

My Journal
Review your answers to the Lesson Preview questions.

196 • Chapter 5   STANDARDS 1.a., 1.b.

Main Ideas

1. How can distance help locate an object? (p. 180)
2. How can you tell that an object is moving? (p. 186)
3. What are two ways to measure motion? (p. 188)

Vocabulary

Choose the correct word from the box.

4. The distance an object moves in a set amount of time
5. A place or location
6. An object's change in position or location
7. The length of space between two people, places, or things

| position (p. 178) |
| distance (p. 180) |
| motion (p. 186) |
| speed (p. 190) |

Using Science Skills

8. You make a graph of the distances that three objects moved. What labels do you use?

9. Critical Thinking You know how far away an object is from another object. But you still can't find it. Explain why.

STANDARDS 1.1.a, 2-d 1.b, 5.1.a, 6.1.b, 7.1.a, 8.4.a, 9.1.a.   197

My Journal tells you to review the questions you answered at the start of the chapter.

Unit Wrap-Up

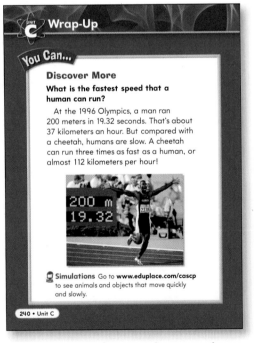

UNIT C Wrap-Up

You Can...

Discover More

What is the fastest speed that a human can run?

At the 1996 Olympics, a man ran 200 meters in 19.32 seconds. That's about 37 kilometers an hour. But compared with a cheetah, humans are slow. A cheetah can run three times as fast as a human, or almost 112 kilometers per hour!

Simulations Go to www.eduplace.com/cascp to see animals and objects that move quickly and slowly.

240 • Unit C

Learn more about science using the Discover More question.

References

Index

Attracts, 246, 248, 250, 252–253, 255, 258–259,

soils and plants of, 149
Steel Venom roller

Picture Glossary

English-Spanish

Health and Fitness Handbook

Science and Math Toolbox

Science and Math Toolbox

Using a Hand Lens H2
Using a Thermometer H3
Using a Ruler H4
Using a Calculator H5
Using a Balance H6
Making a Chart H7
Making a Tally Chart H8
Making a Bar Graph H9

The back of your book includes sections you will refer to again and again.

Start with Your Standards

Your California Science Standards

How Families Can Help. S1

Set 1 Physical Sciences. S2

Set 2 Life Sciences S4

Set 3 Earth Sciences. S5

Set 4 Investigation and Experimentation . . . S6

Your California
Science Standards

Welcome to the adventure of science!

Many famous scientists and inventors have lived and worked in California. You could be one, too!

Your science standards tell you what you should know by the end of Grade 2. They also tell what you should be able to do when you investigate and experiment. You will find the standards printed next to each section of the lesson and chapter.

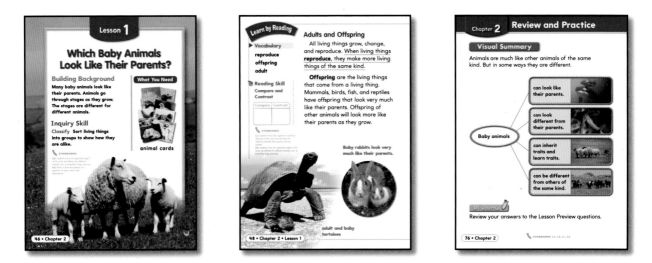

Houghton Mifflin Science will lead you to mastering your standards. Along the way, you will ask questions, do hands-on investigations, think critically, and read what scientists have discovered about how the world works. You will also get to know real people who do science every day.

How Families Can Help

- Get to know the California Science Content Standards on the pages that follow. If you want to learn more about science education, you can find the Science Framework for California Public Schools online at **www.cde.ca.gov/ci/**

- Relate the science of the standards to activities at home such as cooking, gardening, and playing sports.

- Get to know your child's science textbook, encouraging him or her to use the table of contents, index, and glossary. Point out the importance of titles and headings as a means to finding the information needed.

- Help your child choose library books to read about science, nature, inventors, and scientists. You can use the Recommended Literature for Math & Science online database at **www.cde.ca.gov/ci/sc/ll/**

- Find opportunities for your child to use numbers and mathematics skills and to measure and to estimate measurements, such as when planning a trip.

- Encourage your child to do experiments and enter science fairs.

Science Content Standards

These Science Content Standards are learning goals that you will achieve by the end of second grade. Below each standard is the unit or chapter in this book where that standard is taught. In that unit and chapter, there are many opportunities to master the standard—by doing investigations, reading, writing, speaking, and drawing concept maps.

 Set 1

Physical Sciences

The motion of objects can be observed and measured. As a basis for understanding this concept:

Unit C: Motion and Forces
Unit D: Magnets and Sound

1.a. *Students know* the position of an object can be described by locating it in relation to another object or to the background.

Chapter 5: Objects in Motion

1.b. *Students know* an object's motion can be described by recording the change in position of the object over time.

Chapter 5: Objects in Motion

1.c. *Students know* the way to change how something is moving is by giving it a push or a pull. The size of the change is related to the strength, or the amount of force, of the push or pull.

Chapter 6: Forces

1.d. *Students know* tools and machines are used to apply pushes and pulls (forces) to make things move.

Chapter 6: Forces

1.e. *Students know* objects fall to the ground unless something holds them up.

Chapter 6: Forces

1.f. *Students know* magnets can be used to make some objects move without being touched.

Chapter 7: Magnets

1.g. *Students know* sound is made by vibrating objects and can be described by its pitch and volume.

Chapter 8: Making Sound

Los Angeles County Fire Department

Set 2   Life Sciences

Plants and animals have predictable life cycles. As a basis for understanding this concept:

Unit A: Life Cycles

2.a. *Students know* that organisms reproduce offspring of their own kind and that the offspring resemble their parents and one another.

Chapter 1: Plant Life Cycles
Chapter 2: Animal Life Cycles

2.b. *Students know* the sequential stages of life cycles are different for different animals, such as butterflies, frogs, and mice.

Chapter 2: Animal Life Cycles

2.c. *Students know* many characteristics of an organism are inherited from the parents. Some characteristics are caused or influenced by the environment.

Chapter 1: Plant Life Cycles
Chapter 2: Animal Life Cycles

2.d. *Students know* there is variation among individuals of one kind within a population.

Chapter 1: Plant Life Cycles
Chapter 2: Animal Life Cycles

2.e. *Students know* light, gravity, touch, or environmental stress can affect the germination, growth, and development of plants.

Chapter 1: Plant Life Cycles

2.f. *Students know* flowers and fruits are associated with reproduction in plants.

Chapter 1: Plant Life Cycles

Mountain Bluebird

Earth Sciences

Set 3

Earth is made of materials that have distinct properties and provide resources for human activities. As a basis for understanding this concept:

Unit B: Earth's Resources

3.a. *Students know* how to compare the physical properties of different kinds of rocks and know that rock is composed of different combinations of minerals.

Chapter 3: Rocks, Soils, and Fossils
Chapter 4: Using Resources

3.b. *Students know* smaller rocks come from the breakage and weathering of larger rocks.

Chapter 3: Rocks, Soils, and Fossils

3.c. *Students know* that soil is made partly from weathered rock and partly from organic materials and that soils differ in their color, texture, capacity to retain water, and ability to support the growth of many kinds of plants.

Chapter 3: Rocks, Soils, and Fossils
Chapter 4: Using Resources

3.d. *Students know* that fossils provide evidence about the plants and animals that lived long ago and that scientists learn about the past history of Earth by studying fossils.

Chapter 3: Rocks, Soils, and Fossils

3.e. *Students know* rock, water, plants, and soil provide many resources, including food, fuel, and building materials, that humans use.

Chapter 4: Using Resources

Investigation and Experimentation

Scientific progress is made by asking meaningful questions and conducting careful investigations. As a basis for understanding this concept and addressing the content in the other three strands, students should develop their own questions and perform investigations. Students will:

Directed Inquiry and Guided Inquiry investigations in every lesson

4.a. Make predictions based on observed patterns and not random guessing.

Directed Inquiry and Guided Inquiry investigations

4.b. Measure length, weight, temperature, and liquid volume with appropriate tools and express those measurements in standard metric system units.

Directed Inquiry and Guided Inquiry investigations

4.c. Compare and sort common objects according to two or more physical attributes (e.g., color, shape, texture, size, weight).

Directed Inquiry and Guided Inquiry investigations

4.d. Write or draw descriptions of a sequence of steps, events, and observations.

Directed Inquiry and Guided Inquiry investigations

4.e. Construct bar graphs to record data, using appropriately labeled axes.

Directed Inquiry and Guided Inquiry investigations

4.f. Use magnifiers or microscopes to observe and draw descriptions of small objects or small features of objects.

Directed Inquiry and Guided Inquiry investigations

4.g. Follow oral instructions for a scientific investigation.

Directed Inquiry and Guided Inquiry investigations; Alternate Inquiry investigations in the Teacher's Edition

The Nature of Science

Science is an adventure.
People all over the world do
science. You can do science, too.
You probably already do.

Big Idea

Scientific progress is made by asking meaningful questions and conducting careful investigations.

Start With Your Standards

STANDARD SET 4. Investigation and Experimentation

4. Scientific progress is made by asking meaningful questions and conducting careful investigations. As a basis for understanding this concept and addressing the content in the other three strands, students should develop their own questions and perform investigations. Students will:

4.a. Make predictions based on observed patterns and not random guessing.

4.b. Measure length, weight, temperature, and liquid volume with appropriate tools and express those measurements in standard metric system units.

4.c. Compare and sort common objects according to two or more physical attributes (e.g., color, shape, texture, size, weight).

4.d. Write or draw descriptions of a sequence of steps, events, and observations.

4.e. Construct bar graphs to record data, using appropriately labeled axes.

4.f. Use magnifiers or microscopes to observe and draw descriptions of small objects or small features of objects.

4.g. Follow oral instructions for a scientific investigation.

The Nature of Science

You Can Do What Scientists Do   S10

You Can Think Like a Scientist . . S12

You Can Be an Inventor S18

You Can Make Decisions S22

Science Safety S24

Do What Scientists Do

Meet Fernando Caldeiro, the astronaut. His friends call him Frank. He is training to go into space. When he is not training, he tests computer programs used to run the space shuttle. Before Mr. Caldeiro became an astronaut, he tested new jets. He also worked on space shuttle rockets.

Frank Caldeiro is floating in a jet that gives the feeling of low gravity. This jet is one tool scientists use to learn more about space.
The jet's nickname is the "vomit comet." Can you guess why?

Many Kinds of Investigations

Astronauts carry out many investigations in space. Sometimes they observe Earth and take photos. Other times they do experiments. They may test how plants or animals react to low gravity. They share what they find out with other scientists.

Astronauts learn to fly the space shuttle in machines called simulators. They also learn to use space shuttle tools to collect information.

Think Like a Scientist

Everyone can do science.
To think like a scientist you have to:

▶ ask a lot of questions.

▶ find answers by investigating.

▶ work on a team.

▶ compare your ideas to those of others.

What is this lizard doing? Is it sleeping? Is it waiting for insects to fly by? Or, is it doing something else?

Use Critical Thinking

When you know the difference between what you observe and what you think about your observation, you are a critical thinker. A fact is an observation that can be checked to make sure it is true. An opinion is what you think about the facts. When you ask someone, "How do you know that?" you are asking for facts.

The lizard lies under the heat lamp for a while. Then it gets food. **I wonder if it must warm up before it can move around?**

I read that a lizard's body temperature falls when the air cools. It warms itself by lying in the sun.

Science Inquiry

You can use **scientific inquiry** to find answers to your questions about the world around you. Say you have seen crickets in the yard.

Observe It seems like crickets chirp very fast on some nights, but slowly on other nights.

Ask a question I wonder, does the speed of cricket chirping change with temperature?

Form an idea I think crickets chirp faster when it's warmer.

Experiment I will need a timer and a thermometer. I will count how many times a cricket chirps in 2 minutes. I will do this when the air temperature is warmer and when the air temperature is cooler.

Conclusion I counted more chirps in warmer air temperatures. This result supports my idea. Crickets chirp faster when it is warmer.

Scientific inquiry includes communicating what you learn. You can tell about your experiment by writing, drawing, or making bar graphs.

Inquiry Process

Here is a process that some scientists follow to answer questions and make new discoveries.

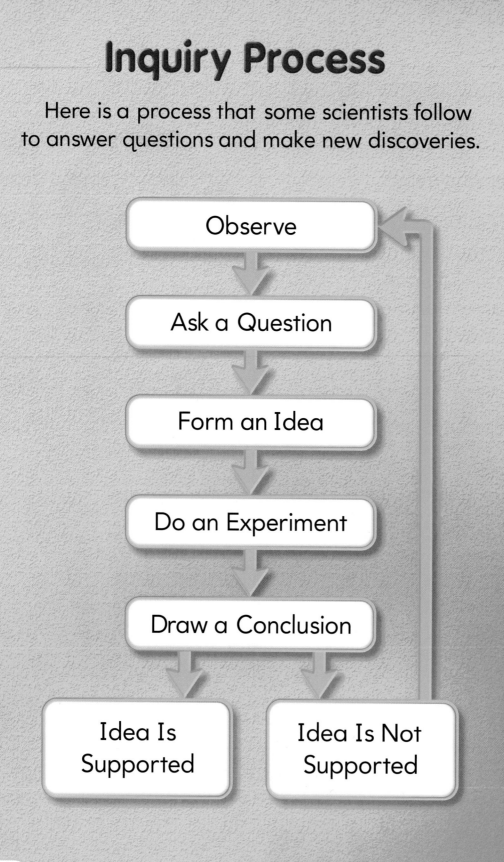

STANDARDS
4.a. Make predictions based on observed patterns and not random guessing.
4.d. Write or draw descriptions of a sequence of steps, events, and observations.

Try it Yourself!

Experiment With Bouncing Balls

Both balls look the same. However, one ball bounces and the other one does not.

 What questions do you have about the balls?

 How would you find out the answers?

③ Write an experiment plan. Tell what you think you will find out.

Be an Inventor

Lloyd French has enjoyed building things and taking them apart since being in the sixth grade in Oakland, California.

Mr. French invents robots. They are used as tools to make observations in places where people cannot easily go. One of his robots can travel to the bottom of the ocean. Another robot, called Cryobot, melts through thick layers of ice—either in Antarctica or on Mars. Cryobot takes photos as it moves through the ice.

"If you want to be a scientist or engineer, it helps to have a sense of curiosity and discovery."

What Is Technology?

The tools people make and use are all technology. A pencil is technology. A cryobot is technology. So is a robot that moves like a human.

Scientists use technology. For example, a microscope makes it possible to see things that cannot be seen with just the eyes. Measurement tools are used to make their observations more exact.

Many technologies make the world a better place to live. But sometimes solving one problem causes others. For example, airplanes make travel faster, but they are noisy and pollute the air.

A Better Idea

"I wish I had a better way to _____".
How would you fill in the blank?
Everyone wishes they could do something
more easily. Inventors try to make those
wishes come true. Inventing or improving
an invention takes time and patience.

Kids have been riding
on scooters for many
years. These newer
scooters are faster.
The tires won't get
flat. They are also
easier to carry from
place to place.

How to Be an Inventor

1. **Find a problem.** It may be at school, at home, or in your community.

2. **Think of a way to solve the problem.** List different ways to solve the problem. Decide which one will work best.

3. **Make a sample and try your invention.** Your idea may need many materials or none at all. Each time you try it, record how it works.

4. **Improve your invention.** Use what you learned to make your design better.

5. **Share your invention.** Draw or write about your invention. Tell how it makes an activity easier or more fun. If it did not work well, tell why.

Make Decisions

Plastic Litter and Ocean Animals

It is a windy day at the beach. A plastic bag blows out of sight. It may float in the ocean for years.

Plastic litter can harm ocean animals. Sometimes sea turtles mistake floating plastic bags for jellyfish, their favorite food. The plastic blocks the stomach, and food cannot get in. Pelicans and dolphins get tangled up in fishing line, six-pack rings, and packaging materials. Sometimes they get so tangled that they cannot move.

Deciding What to Do

How can ocean animals be protected from plastic litter?

Here's how to make your decision. You can use the same steps to help solve problems in your home, in your school, and in your community.

 Learn → Learn about the problem. You could talk to an expert, read a science book, or explore a web site.

 **List** → Make a list of actions you could take. Add actions other people could take.

 **Decide** → Decide which action is best for you or your community.

 Share → Explain your decision to others.

Science Safety

Know the safety rules of your classroom and follow them. Read and follow the safety tips in your science book.

- ▶ Wear safety goggles when your teacher tells you.

- ▶ Keep your work area clean. Tell your teacher about spills right away.

- ▶ Learn how to care for the plants and animals in your classroom.

- ▶ Wash your hands when you are done.

Life Cycles

California Connection

Visit www.eduplace.com/cascp to find out more about the life cycles of California plants and animals.

California Field Trip

Sequoia National Park

Giant Sequoias need
thousands of gallons of
water a day to grow.

Jeffrey shooting star flowers grow along stream banks and in wet meadows.

California newts eat earthworms, snails, and slugs.

LIFE SCIENCE · UNIT A

Life Cycles

Reading in Science 2

Chapter 1
Plant Life Cycles 4

Independent Books
- Plant Life Cycles
- Ynes Mexia, Plant Collector
- The Life of a Bean

Chapter 2
Animal Life Cycles 42

Independent Books
- Animal Life Cycles
- Are They Look-Alikes?
- The Animal Trackers

California sea lions

Standard Set 2.
Life Sciences

Plants and animals have predictable life cycles.

Caterpillar

by Mary Dawson

Creepy crawly caterpillar
Looping up and down,
Furry tufts of hair along
Your back of golden brown.

You will soon be wrapped in silk,
Asleep for many a day;
And then, a handsome butterfly,
You'll stretch and fly away.

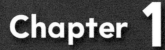

Plant Life Cycles

Pink water lilies

LESSON
1
Seeds form in fruits. How are seeds important to plants?

LESSON
2

Corn seeds come from a corn plant. What grows if you plant a corn seed?

LESSON
3
Not all daisies look alike. How might daisies in a field be different?

LESSON
4

This plant is growing toward the window. Why would this happen?

My Journal

Write or draw in your journal to answer the questions above.

Vocabulary Preview

Vocabulary

flower p. 10

fruit p. 10

seed p. 10

life cycle p. 12

cone p. 14

inherit p. 20

environment p. 27

population p. 28

gravity p. 34

Picture Glossary
English-Spanish p. H18

Vocabulary Skill

Use Syllables

environment

Break the word into syllables. Say each syllable aloud, clapping once for each syllable.

flower
A flower is a plant part where fruit and seeds form.

cone
A cone is the part where seeds form in a plant without flowers.

population
A population is a group of the same kind of living thing in one place.

environment

An environment is all the living and nonliving things around a living thing.

Start with Your Standards

Standard Set 2. Life Sciences

2.a. *Students know* that organisms reproduce offspring of their own kind and that the offspring resemble their parents and one another.

2.c. *Students know* many characteristics of an organism are inherited from the parents. Some characteristics are caused or influenced by the environment.

2.d. *Students know* there is variation among individuals of one kind within a population.

2.e. *Students know* light, gravity, touch, or environmental stress can affect the germination, growth, and development of plants.

2.f. *Students know* flowers and fruits are associated with reproduction in plants.

Standard Set 4. Investigation and Experimentation covered in this chapter: 4.d., 4.e., 4.f., 4.g.

How Do Plants Change During Their Life Cycles?

Building Background

Fruits and seeds form inside a flower. New plants grow from seeds.

Inquiry Skill

Observe You can use a hand lens to see small objects or details.

What You Need

fruits

hand lens

crayons

STANDARDS

2.f. *Students know* flowers and fruits are associated with reproduction in plants.
4.f. Use magnifiers or microscopes to observe and draw descriptions of small objects or small features of objects.

Fruits and Seeds

Steps

STEP 1

1 **Observe** Look at the outside of each fruit. Draw a picture of what you see. **Safety:** Do not eat the fruit!

2 **Observe** Use a hand lens to look closely at the inside of each fruit. Draw a picture of what you see. **Safety:** Wash your hands!

STEP 2

3 **Communicate** Share your drawings with others. Talk about what you saw.

STEP 3

Think and Share

1. **Compare** How were all the fruits alike?

2. **Infer** What would you find if you cut open a different fruit?

Guided Inquiry

Experiment Think of some seeds that you can open with your fingers. Open them. **Observe** and record what is inside. Compare what is inside different seeds.

Vocabulary

flower

fruit

seed

life cycle

cone

Reading Skill

Sequence

First
↓
Next
↓
Last

STANDARDS

2.f. *Students know* flowers and fruits are associated with reproduction in plants.

Plant Parts

A plant has many parts. Some parts help a plant make new plants. A **flower** is the plant part where fruit and seeds form. A **fruit** is the part of a flower that is around a seed. A **seed** is the part from which a new plant grows.

Pea Plant

Inside a seed is a new plant and the food it needs to grow.

flower

seed

fruit

Pea plants and almond trees have flowers. Both kinds of flowers have seeds inside. The flowers dry up after the fruit and seeds form. The fruits grow bigger. If the seeds are planted in soil, they can grow into new plants.

flower

Sequence What happens after the fruit and seeds form?

Sweet Almond Tree

fruit

seed

Express Lab

Activity Card 1
Order a Plant Life Cycle

Plant Life Cycles

All living things grow, change, and finally die. The series of changes that a living thing goes though as it grows is its **life cycle**.

Different kinds of plants have different life cycles. Most plants start from a seed. When the seed gets what it needs, it starts to grow.

Tomato Plant

Seeds fall into soil. They need warmth and water to sprout.

The young plant's roots grow down. The stem grows up.

The plant changes as it grows. The adult plant makes flowers.

The plant grows and changes. It grows more stems and leaves. It grows flowers that make new seeds and fruit. New plants can grow from the seeds. These plants will look like the parent plant from which they came. The cycle of growing and changing starts again.

Sequence **When does a seed start to grow?**

Flowers make fruit. Seeds grow inside the fruit.

The parent plant dies. The seeds may scatter. They may grow into new plants.

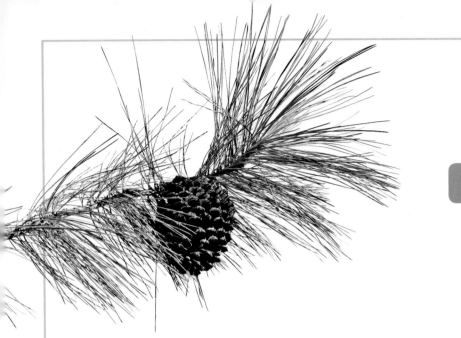

Pine Tree

Pine seeds grow in a cone.

A seed grows into a young plant called a seedling.

Life Cycle of a Pine Tree

Not all plants have flowers and fruits. Some plants have cones. A **cone** is the part where seeds form in plants without flowers. The cone protects the seeds while they grow.

Sequence How does a pine tree change as it grows?

The seedling grows into a tree.

The tree grows and cones form.

The life cycle begins again with new seeds.

Lesson Wrap-Up

❶ **Vocabulary** What is a **seed**?

❷ 🎯 **Reading Skill** What stage comes after the seed in a plant's life cycle?

❸ **Observe** How does a hand lens help you observe seeds?

Technology Visit www.eduplace.com/cascp to find out more about plant life cycles.

STANDARDS 1–3: 2.f.

EXTREME Science

What's the BiG Stink?

Whoa! That smells!

This giant flower smells like rotten meat! The titan arum's powerful smell attracts meat-eating beetles. The beetles move from flower to flower looking for food. A powder in the flower sticks to the legs of the beetle. The powder drops off the beetle's legs in the next flower. The flowers use the powder to make seeds.

The titan arum has one of the biggest, stinkiest flowers in the world.

The titan arum can measure 1 meter across and up to 3 meters tall.

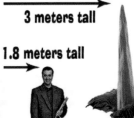

How TALL is it?

3 meters tall

1.8 meters tall

My Journal

Write in your journal about how the flower of the titan arum is important for the growth of new plants.

What Kind of a Plant Grows from a Seed?

Building Background

A parent plant makes new plants of the same kind. It passes along traits, such as shape and color, to the new plant.

Inquiry Skill

Compare Tell how objects or events are alike and different.

STANDARDS

2.c. *Students know* many characteristics of an organism are inherited from the parents. Some characteristics are caused or influenced by the environment.
4.d. Write or draw descriptions of a sequence of steps, events, and observations.

What You Need

goggles

seeds

cup and soil

water and ruler

Plant Seeds

Steps

1. Choose one kind of seed. Look at the picture on the packet. Plant several seeds in soil. Water as needed. **Safety:** Wear goggles!

STEP 1

2. **Observe** Watch for a plant to start to grow. Draw that plant every day. Use a chart like the one shown.

STEP 2

Plant Growth

Date	Date	Date	Date	Date
Height	Height	Height	Height	Height
Date	Date	Date	Date	Date
Height	Height	Height	Height	Height

3. **Measure** Measure your plant every day. Record its height below each drawing. **Safety:** Wash your hands!

STEP 3

Think and Share

1. **Compare** How is your plant like the plant pictured on the seed packet? How is it different?

2. **Infer** Why does your plant look like the one on the seed packet?

Guided Inquiry

Ask Questions Think about how plants are alike and different. Ask: What if I planted a _____ seed? **Predict** what would happen.

► **Vocabulary**

inherit

◎ **Reading Skill**

Draw Conclusions

STANDARDS

2.a. *Students know* that organisms reproduce offspring of their own kind and that the offspring resemble their parents and one another.
2.c. *Students know* many characteristics of an organism are inherited from the parents. Some characteristics are caused or influenced by the environment.

Plants and Their Parents

New plants grow from the seeds of the parent plant. The new plant inherits traits from the parent plant. All living things **inherit**, or have passed on to them, traits from their parents.

Some traits that a plant may inherit are color, shape, or size. The new plant will have the same leaf shape as the parent plant. It will grow the same kind of fruit. The new plant may be the same color as the parent plant. It may grow to be the same size.

When new California poppies grow, they look like the parent plants.

How Plants Compare

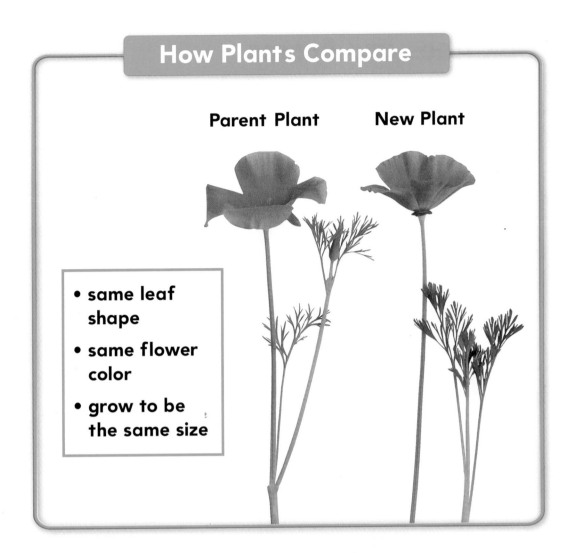

Parent Plant   **New Plant**

- same leaf shape
- same flower color
- grow to be the same size

🎯 **Draw Conclusions** In what ways might a new tulip plant be like its parent plant?

Express Lab

Activity Card 2
Compare Young Plants to Their Parents

Oak Trees and Acorns

Acorns are the fruit of an oak tree. When acorns fall to the ground, the seeds inside may grow into new plants.

acorns

Blue Oak Tree

The new plants look like one another and like the parent plant. They are all oak trees. They all inherit the same flat leaves. Like their parent, the new oak plants may someday form acorns. The seeds inside the acorns may grow into new oak trees.

new oak trees

 **Draw Conclusions** What kinds of plants always grow from acorns?

Lesson Wrap-Up

❶ **Vocabulary** What do new plants **inherit**?

❷ **Reading Skill** What would the seeds of a maple tree grow into?

❸ **Compare** How is a new plant like its parent plant?

Technology Visit **www.eduplace.com/cascp** to find out more about plants.

STANDARDS 1–3: 2.a., 2.c.

How Do Plants of the Same Kind Differ?

Building Background

Plants of the same kind are not exactly alike. They may be different sizes or colors.

Inquiry Skill

Use Numbers Use numbers to describe and compare objects.

STANDARDS

2.d. *Students know* there is variation among individuals of one kind within a population.
4.e. Construct bar graphs to record data, using appropriately labeled axes.

What You Need

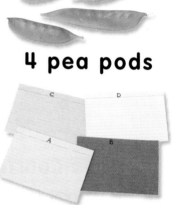

4 pea pods

4 index cards

crayons and ruler

Peas in Pod

bar graph

Compare Pea Pods

Steps

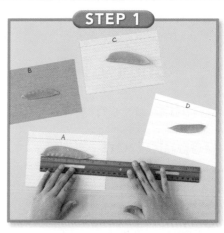
STEP 1

① **Measure** Put a pea pod on each index card. Measure the length of each pod in centimeters. Record your data on the cards.

STEP 2

② **Record Data** Open pod **A**. Count the number of peas. Record the number on the card. Repeat for each pod.

STEP 3

③ **Use Numbers** Complete the bar graph. Add labels. Use the data on the cards to graph the number of peas in each pod.

Think and Share

1. **Use Numbers** How do the lengths of the pods compare? How do the number of peas compare?

2. **Predict** What do you think you would find if you looked at four more pea pods? Tell why.

Guided Inquiry

Experiment Measure the length of three bananas or apples. Use a balance to **measure** the mass of each fruit. How are fruits of the same kind different?

environment

population

◎ **Reading Skill**
Compare and Contrast

Different | Alike | Different

STANDARDS

2.d. *Students know* there is variation among individuals of one kind within a population.
2.c. Students know many characteristics of an organism are inherited from the parents. Some characteristics are caused or influenced by the environment.

The Same but Different

You learned that new plants inherit traits from the parent plant. The new plants often look like the parents and one another.

But new plants that grow from seeds from the same parent are not exactly alike. The new plants may be different because they may inherit different traits. Their size may be different. They may even be a different color.

Seeds from a red raspberry plant may produce new plants that make red or gold raspberries.

What might cause these two new plants to look different?

There are other reasons that new plants from the same parents may look different. The plants may be affected by their environment.

An **environment** is all the living and nonliving things around a living thing. A new plant that does not get the right amount of sunlight may not grow as well as others.

Compare and Contrast In what ways can new plants from the same parents differ?

Express Lab

Activity Card 3
Compare Leaf Size

a population
of petunias

Differences in a Bigger Group

You can see differences among plants from the same parents. You can see even more differences among plants of a population. A **population** is a group of the same kind of living thing in one place.

All the petunia plants in a garden make up a population. The plants may inherit different traits. They may have flowers of different shapes and colors, but they are all part of the same population. They are all petunias.

Each daffodil inherited different traits from its parent plants.

Plants in a population can also look different because they are affected by their environment. A plant that has more space will grow better than one that is crowded. Plants that get too much water will not grow well.

How are these plants affected by their environment?

Compare and Contrast How might plants of a population be the same and different?

Lesson Wrap-Up

❶ **Vocabulary** What is a **population**?

❷ **Reading Skill** How might new plants of the same parents be the same and different?

❸ **Use Numbers** How can you use numbers to describe differences between two plants?

Technology Visit www.eduplace.com/cascp to find out more about plant differences.

STANDARDS 1: 2.d., 2: 2.c., 3: 2.d.

Great Grapes

In the 1870s, William Thompson and his son, George, grew the first seedless grapes in Yuba County, California. People liked the seedless grapes. Since then, grape growers have created many kinds of seedless grapes.

Grape growers choose plants with the traits that people like. Growers use seeds or stem cuttings from those plants to grow new plants. The new plants inherit traits from the parent plants.

Most California raisins are made from Thompson seedless grapes.

STANDARDS

2.c. *Students know* many characteristics of an organism are inherited from the parents. Some characteristics are caused or influenced by the environment.
2.d. *Students know* there is variation among individuals of one kind within a population.

READING  L I N K

All of the seedless grapes in California are offspring of the grapes that Thompson grew in the 1870s. Red Flame seedless grapes were created by combining Thompson seedless grapes with some other kinds of grapes.

Sharing Ideas

1. **Write About It** How do grape growers create new kinds of grapes?

2. **Talk About It** Describe a new kind of fruit that you would like to grow. What traits would it have?

How Do Plants React to Their Environment?

Building Background

A plant's environment can affect the way it grows.

Inquiry Skill

Record Data You can write or draw what happens first, next, and last.

STANDARDS

2.e. *Students know* light, gravity, touch, or environmental stress can affect the germination, growth, and development of plants.
4.g. Follow oral instructions for a scientific investigation.

What You Need

seeds

2 plastic bags
and paper towels

thermometer
and water

chart

Sprouting Seeds

Steps

1 Put a wet paper towel and four seeds in each bag. Put one bag in a refrigerator. Put the other bag in a dark closet.

STEP 1

2 **Measure** Measure the temperature of the air next to each bag. Record the data in a chart.

STEP 2

3 **Record Data** Observe the seeds. Record in the chart what you see.

4 Repeat steps 2 and 3 every day for one week.

STEP 3

Seed Growth			
Day	Temperature in Refrigerator	Temperature in Closet	Observations
Monday	5°C	20°C	

Think and Share

1. **Compare** Which seeds sprouted and grew faster?

2. **Predict** What might happen if you moved the seeds that were in the refrigerator to the closet?

Guided Inquiry

Experiment Think of a plan to **compare** how plants grow in different amounts of light. Tell your plan to a classmate. Have the classmate follow your plan.

▶ **Vocabulary**

gravity

◎ **Reading Skill**

Cause and Effect

Cause ➔ Effect

▶ **STANDARDS**

2.e. *Students know* light, gravity, touch, or environmental stress can affect the germination, growth, and development of plants.

Gravity, Light, and Touch

Plants are affected by gravity, light, and touch. **Gravity** is a force that causes objects to fall to the ground unless something holds them up.

The roots of a plant grow down toward the pull of gravity. As the roots grow down into the soil, the plant gets the water it needs. The stems of a plant grow up, away from the pull of gravity.

How is this tree affected by gravity?

A mimosa plant reacts to the touch of a pencil.

Some plants are affected by touch. A mimosa plant closes its leaves when it is touched. It protects itself from danger. When insects crawl on the leaves, the leaves close. The insects cannot eat the leaves and go away.

A plant needs sunlight to make food. So the stem of a plant grows toward the light. People sometimes turn their houseplants a little each day. This helps the stems grow straight.

How is this plant affected by light?

Cause and Effect How does gravity affect plants?

Express Lab

Activity Card 4
Compare Temperature

Weather Affects Plants

<u>Weather can affect how plants grow.</u> Air temperature, wind, and rainfall all affect plant growth.

Strong, sudden wind can cause trees and crops to fall over. Wind might also pull some plants out of the soil. Steady winds can change the shape of a growing tree over time.

This pine tree in the Sierra Nevada mountains was affected by the wind.

If the temperature gets too hot or too cold, plants can be injured or die. Very hot weather can cause plants to stop growing.

The wrong amount of water can affect how plants grow. If there is too little rain, seeds will not start to grow. If there is too much rain, a plant's roots might rot.

A quick drop in temperature injured this plant.

 **Cause and Effect** How can weather affect how plants grow?

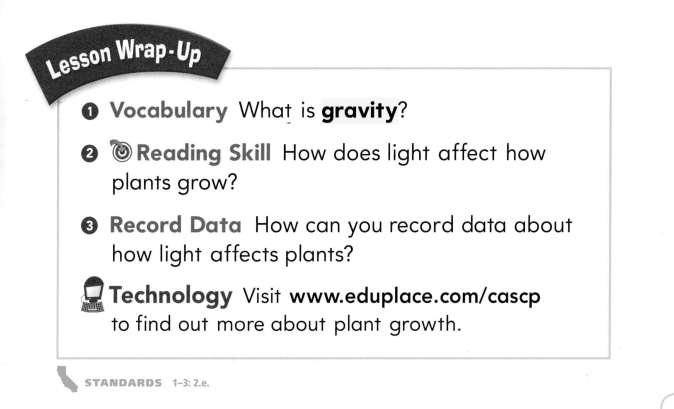

Lesson Wrap-Up

❶ **Vocabulary** What is **gravity**?

❷ **Reading Skill** How does light affect how plants grow?

❸ **Record Data** How can you record data about how light affects plants?

Technology Visit **www.eduplace.com/cascp** to find out more about plant growth.

STANDARDS 1–3: 2.e.

Math Compare Seeds

Keesha and Mark each have a pumpkin. They open the pumpkins and count the seeds inside. The chart shows their results.

Pumpkin Seeds	
Child	Number of Seeds
Keesha	85
Mark	62

1. Compare the number of seeds. Use the symbols < or >.

2. Whose pumpkin has more seeds? How many more seeds does it have?

Writing Describe a Plant

Write about a kind of plant that you know. Tell how the plant changes as it grows. Start with a seed. Draw pictures to go with your story. Then share your story with the class.

How My Seed Grows

Botanist

A botanist is a scientist who studies plants. Some botanists try to grow new kinds of plants. Some look for new plants in the wild.

Some botanists work with farmers. They look for ways to keep harmful insects away from plants. They also find ways for farmers to grow more crops.

What It Takes!

- At least four years of college
- An interest in science and plants

Visual Summary

The way plants grow and change depends on the parent plants and the environment.

Seeds form in fruits.

Plants inherit many traits from the parents.

Plants Grow and Change

Plants in the same population can be different.

Plants are affected by their environment.

My Journal

Review your answers to the Lesson Preview questions.

STANDARDS 2.a., 2.c., 2.d., 2.e., 2.f.

Main Ideas

1. What are three parts of a plant that help make new plants? (p. 10)

2. List two reasons why new plants with the same parents might be different. (pp. 26–27)

3. Explain why the roots of a bush grow down and its stem grows up. (pp. 34–35)

Vocabulary

Choose the correct word from the box.

4. A group of the same kind of living thing in one place

5. A plant part where fruit and seeds form

6. All the living and nonliving things around a living thing

7. The part of a flower that is around a seed

flower (p. 10)
fruit (p. 10)
environment (p. 27)
population (p. 28)

Using Science Skills

8. Describe the stages of a plant's life cycle.

9. **Critical Thinking** A new tree and its parent plant have the same color bark. Explain why.

STANDARDS 1: 2.f., 2: 2.c., 3: 2.e., 4: 2.d., 5: 2.f., 6: 2.c., 2.e., 7: 2.f., 8: 2.f., 4.d., 9: 2.a., 2.c.

Animal Life Cycles

Mother swan and baby

Lesson Preview

LESSON 1

These chicks look alike. How are they like their parents?

LESSON 2

A caterpillar changes as it grows. How does it change?

LESSON 3

This dog can fetch. Why can some dogs do tricks?

LESSON 4

These hamsters are alike in many ways. How are they different?

My Journal

Write or draw in your journal to answer the questions above.

Vocabulary

reproduce p. 48

offspring p. 48

adult p. 49

larva p. 56

pupa p. 56

learned p. 62

individual p. 69

Picture Glossary
English-Spanish p. H18

Vocabulary Skill

Use What's Before

reproduce

The prefix **re-** means again. **Produce** means to make. So reproduce means to make again.

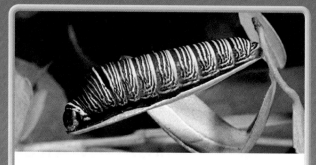

larva

A larva is the worm-like stage in an insect's life cycle.

pupa

A pupa is the stage when an insect changes form.

learned

Traits that are learned are not passed on from parents to their offspring.

reproduce

When living things reproduce, they make more living things of the same kind.

Start with Your Standards

Standard Set 2. Life Sciences

2.a. *Students know* that organisms reproduce offspring of their own kind and that the offspring resemble their parents and one another.

2.b. *Students know* the sequential stages of life cycles are different for different animals, such as butterflies, frogs, and mice.

2.c. *Students know* many characteristics of an organism are inherited from the parents. Some characteristics are caused or influenced by the environment.

2.d. *Students know* there is variation among individuals of one kind within a population.

Standard Set 4. Investigation and Experimentation covered in this chapter: 4.a., 4.b., 4.d., 4.f.

Which Baby Animals Look Like Their Parents?

Building Background

Many baby animals look like their parents. Animals go through stages as they grow. The stages are different for different animals.

Inquiry Skill

Classify Sort living things into groups to show how they are alike.

STANDARDS

2.b. *Students know* the sequential stages of life cycles are different for different animals, such as butterflies, frogs, and mice.
4.d. Write or draw descriptions of a sequence of steps, events, and observations.

What You Need

animal cards

Compare Life Cycles

Steps

1 **Observe** Look at the animal pictures. Name the animals.

2 **Classify** Think about how the animal pictures are alike and different. Sort the pictures. Make a group for each kind of animal.

3 Order each group. Put the baby first and the adult animal last.

4 **Record Data** Choose one group. Use the pictures to write about or draw the life cycle of that animal.

STEP 1

STEP 2

STEP 3

Think and Share

1. **Compare** How are the baby and adult in each group alike?

2. How do some animals change from babies to adults?

Guided Inquiry

Ask Questions Write three questions about how animals grow and change. **Work together** with classmates to find the answers.

47

Vocabulary

reproduce

offspring

adult

Reading Skill

Compare and Contrast

Compare	Contrast

STANDARDS

2.a. *Students know* that organisms reproduce offspring of their own kind and that the offspring resemble their parents and one another.

2.b. *Students know* the sequential stages of life cycles are different for different animals, such as butterflies, frogs, and mice.

Adults and Offspring

All living things grow, change, and reproduce. When living things **reproduce**, they make more living things of the same kind.

Offspring are the living things that come from a living thing. Mammals, birds, fish, and reptiles have offspring that look very much like their parents. Offspring of other animals will look more like their parents as they grow.

Baby rabbits look very much like their parents.

adult and baby tortoises

Offspring grow and change during their lives. A baby penguin will become a full grown penguin. An animal that is full grown is an **adult**. Then it will be about the same size and color as its parent. The series of changes that an animal goes through as it grows is its life cycle.

adult and baby penguins

🎯 **Compare and Contrast** How are parents and offspring alike and different?

How do this adult and baby orca whale look alike?

Express Lab

Activity Card 5
Match Animals

49

Life Cycle of a Bird

A mother bird lays eggs. A chick grows inside each one.

A chick hatches from an egg. A parent feeds it.

Life Cycle of a Mouse

A mother mouse gives birth to baby mice.

The mother's body makes milk. The babies drink the milk.

Familiar Life Cycles

The stages in a life cycle are different for different animals. A mouse is a mammal. A mammal is born alive. A bird hatches from an egg. Baby birds and baby mice are much like their parents.

🎯 **Compare and Contrast** How are the life cycles of a bird and a mouse the same?

The chick gets new feathers as it grows.

The young bird grows to be an adult. It can reproduce.

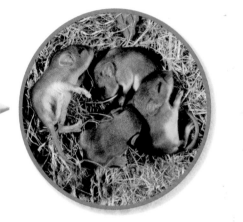

The mice grow more fur. They get bigger.

This mouse is fully grown. As an adult, it can reproduce.

Lesson Wrap-Up

❶ **Vocabulary** What is an **offspring**?

❷ **⦿ Reading Skill** How is the life cycle of a bird different from that of a mouse?

❸ **Classify** How could you sort animals by their life cycles?

Technology Visit **www.eduplace.com/cascp** to find out more about animal life cycles.

Which Baby Animals Look Unlike Their Parents?

Building Background

Some young animals do not look like their parents. The young animals change form as they grow.

Inquiry Skill

Use Data You can use what you observe and record to learn more about something.

STANDARDS

2.b. *Students know* the sequential stages of life cycles are different for different animals, such as butterflies, frogs, and mice.
4.f. Use magnifiers or microscopes to observe and draw descriptions of small objects or small features of objects.

What You Need

Triops tank

Triops eggs

hand lens

ruler

Triops Stages

Steps

1. Gently pour the Triops eggs into a tank of water.
Safety: Wash your hands!

STEP 1

2. **Observe** Use a hand lens to observe the Triops each day. Draw what they look like.

STEP 2

3. **Measure** When a Triops is three days old, measure its length. Repeat each day for five days. Record each day's data in a table.

STEP 3

Length of Triops	
Day 1	about _____ cm
Day 2	about _____ cm
Day 3	about _____ cm
Day 4	about _____ cm
Day 5	about _____ cm

Think and Share

1. **Use Data** How did the Triops change over time?

2. **Infer** How is a baby Triops different from its parents?

Guided Inquiry

Ask Questions Look at the chart of a partner. **Compare** your data. If your data is different, ask questions about why your data is different.

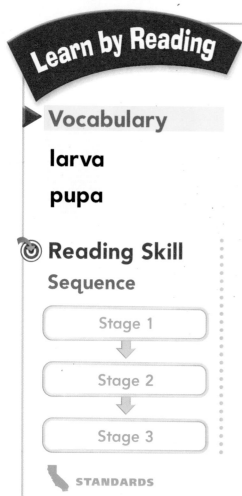

Vocabulary

larva

pupa

Reading Skill

Sequence

Stage 1

↓

Stage 2

↓

Stage 3

STANDARDS

2.b. *Students know* the sequential stages of life cycles are different for different animals, such as butterflies, frogs, and mice.

Frog Life Cycle

Some young animals look very different from their parents. These animals change form as they grow to be adults.

Most amphibians change form as they grow. When they become adults, they will look like their parents.

Life Cycle of a Frog

A frog lays its eggs in water.

A tadpole hatches from an egg. It has gills, a tail, and no legs.

Over many weeks, a tadpole's back legs grow. Its skin gets thicker.

A frog is an amphibian. When frogs hatch from eggs, they have body parts that help them live in water.

Later, frogs grow parts that will help them live on land. Parts that they needed to live in water disappear. When frogs become adults, they look like their parents.

Sequence What happens after parts for living on land form?

Lungs grow and gills disappear. The tail will soon disappear.

The tadpole grows to be an adult frog. An adult frog can reproduce.

Express Lab

Activity Card 6
Measure How a Frog Changes

55

A butterfly lays eggs on a plant.

A larva hatches from an egg. It eats the plant it is on.

A pupa does not eat. Wings and legs are forming.

Butterfly Life Cycle

Butterflies are insects. Most insects change form as they grow. The first stage in the life cycle of most insects is the egg. A larva hatches from the egg. A **larva** is the worm-like stage in an insect's life cycle. It looks very different from its parents.

A larva grows and sheds its skin many times. Then it turns into a pupa. A **pupa** is the stage when an insect changes form.

The change is finished. The pupa has become a butterfly.

A butterfly lives for several weeks. It lays eggs, and a new life cycle begins.

Sequence What stage follows the larva stage?

Lesson Wrap-Up

1. **Vocabulary** What is a **larva**?

2. **Reading Skill** What happens before a tadpole's back legs grow?

3. **Use Data** How is the data that you collect about life cycles useful?

Technology Visit **www.eduplace.com/cascp** to find out more about animals that change form.

Where Do Animals Get Their Traits?

Building Background

Animals inherit many traits from their parents. Some traits are learned or caused by the environment.

Inquiry Skill

Predict Instead of guessing, use patterns you observe to tell what you think will happen.

goldfish

pencil

fish food

STANDARDS

2.c. *Students know* many characteristics of an organism are inherited from the parents. Some characteristics are caused or influenced by the environment.
4.a. Make predictions based on observed patterns and not random guessing.

Train Goldfish

Steps

STEP 1

1. **Experiment** Use a pencil to gently tap a signal at one end of a fish tank. Watch and record what the fish do. Feed the fish at the other end of the tank.

STEP 2

2. **Record Data** Repeat Step 1 for the next three days. Watch and record what the fish do.

3. **Predict** On the fifth day, predict what the fish will do when you tap on the tank. Test your prediction, but do not feed the fish. Watch and record the actions of the fish.

STEP 3

Think and Share

1. **Infer** How did using the signal when you fed the fish help train them?

2. **Predict** What might happen if you tried this with different fish?

Guided Inquiry

Experiment Think about ways to train other animals. Make a plan. Communicate your plan with classmates.

▶ **Vocabulary**

learned

◎ **Reading Skill**
Draw Conclusions

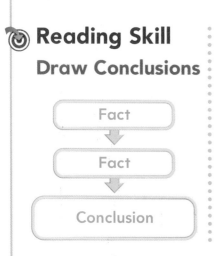

STANDARDS

2.a. *Students know* that organisms reproduce offspring of their own kind and that the offspring resemble their parents and one another.
2.c. *Students know* many characteristics of an organism are inherited from the parents. Some characteristics are caused or influenced by the environment.

Inherited Traits

Just as new plants inherit traits from their parent plants, young animals inherit traits from their parents. When living things reproduce, they make more living things of the same kind.

When dogs reproduce, they always give birth to puppies. Cats always give birth to kittens, not puppies.

These kittens inherited their body shape from their parents.

How are these children like their parents?

People always give birth to children. Children of the same parents often look alike. They are all children in the same family, but they are all different from one another. They may have different eye or hair color. The shape of their noses may not be the same.

Draw Conclusions Why might a brother and sister have the same ear shape?

Express Lab

Activity Card 7
Observe a Learned Behavior

Learned Traits

Some traits are learned. Traits that are **learned** are not passed on from parents to their offspring. You were not born knowing how to read. Reading is something that is learned.

Like you, animals also learn things as they live. These learned traits will not be passed on to their offspring.

This skunk learned where to find food.

Border collie herding sheep

Some animals are trained to help people. Different animals are trained to do different things.

This monkey has learned to use a CD player.

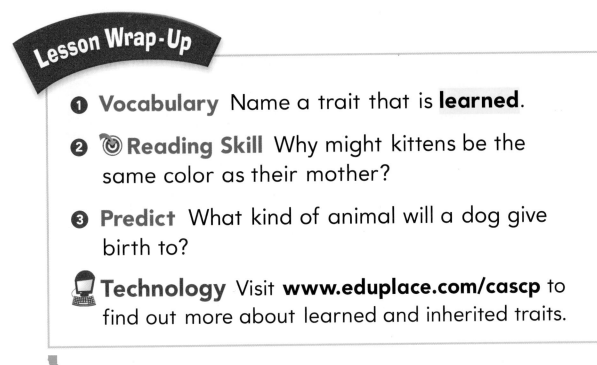

Draw Conclusions Where might a dog get its traits?

Lesson Wrap-Up

① **Vocabulary** Name a trait that is **learned**.

② **Reading Skill** Why might kittens be the same color as their mother?

③ **Predict** What kind of animal will a dog give birth to?

Technology Visit **www.eduplace.com/cascp** to find out more about learned and inherited traits.

EXTREME Science

STANDARDS 2.c. *Students know* many characteristics of an organism are inherited from the parents. Some characteristics are caused or influenced by the environment.

Check Out These Chickens

This breed of Polish hen has been raised for the last 500 years.

Have you ever seen chickens like these? They aren't wearing funny hats! They are bred to have certain traits, such as fluffy, curly feathers.

Breeders choose adult chickens with unusual colors or feathers to reproduce. Offspring that have those traits are chosen to reproduce again. Over time, the traits become common in that group.

This hen got her head feathers from her father and her body feathers from her mother.

The Polish ▶ crested rooster is known for the unusual feathers on its head.

My Journal

Draw your own fancy chicken. Write about which features come from the mother and which features come from the father.

65

How Do Animals of the Same Kind Differ?

Building Background

Living things of the same kind look very much alike. But each one is a little bit different.

Inquiry Skill

Measure Use tools and metric units to find length.

STANDARDS

2.d. *Students know* there is variation among individuals of one kind within a population.
4.b. Measure length, weight, temperature, and liquid volume with appropriate tools and express those measurements in standard metric system units.

What You Need

ruler

paper and pencil

graph

Measure Handspans

Steps

STEP 1

1. **Measure** Spread your fingers and place your hand on a sheet of paper. Draw lines at the end of your little finger and at the end of your thumb. Measure the distance between the two marks. Record your handspan measurement.

2. **Use Numbers** Survey your classmates. Find out each child's handspan. Record data on a tally chart like the one shown.

STEP 2

Handspans	
Measurement	Number of Children
13 Centimeters	
14 Centimeters	
15 Centimeters	
16 Centimeters	
17 Centimeters	
18 Centimeters	
19 Centimeters	

3. **Record Data** Use data from the tally chart to complete the bar graph. Add labels.

STEP 3

Think and Share

1. **Use Numbers** What were the smallest and largest measurements?

2. **Compare** How are hands alike and different?

Guided Inquiry

Experiment Make a plan to compare foot lengths. Use numbers to compare foot measurements to handspan measurements.

67

▶ **Vocabulary**

individual

◎ **Reading Skill**
Main Idea and Details

Main Idea

Detail   Detail

STANDARDS

2.d. *Students know* there is variation among individuals of one kind within a population.
2.a. *Students know* that organisms reproduce offspring of their own kind and that the offspring resemble their parents and one another.

Families Differ

Young animals in a family often look like their parents and one another. But the animals in a family are not exactly alike. Each animal inherits slightly different traits from its parents. The color or size of each animal may be different. They may even act in different ways.

These puppies do not look exactly like their mother.

Comparing Animals

Dark Fur			
Light Fur			
Brown Eyes			
Blue Eyes			

An **individual** is one living thing in a group of the same kind of living things. The table shows how the traits of individuals in a family of dogs compare.

Main Idea How do the animals in a family compare?

Activity Card 8
Compare Two Individuals

69

Animals in a Population Differ

Like animals in a family, animals in a population are not exactly alike. You learned that a population is a group of the same kind of living thing in one place.

Just like animals in a family, animals in a population are different because they inherit different traits. Their size may be different. Their height may be different. They may be a different color. Look at the horses shown below. Each one has different traits, but they all are horses.

a population of horses

Animals from the same parents may look different for another reason. The environment may affect the animals. An animal may not get the same amount of food as another. An animal may get too much food. If an animal gets sick, it may not grow to be as large as others in the population.

🎯 **Main Idea** How can animals in the same population differ?

These individual horses look different, but they are part of the same population.

Lesson Wrap-Up

❶ **Vocabulary** What is an **individual**?

❷ 🎯 **Reading Skill** List two ways that animals from one family may be alike.

❸ **Measure** How can measuring show differences in animals?

💻 **Technology** Visit **www.eduplace.com/cascp** to find out more about animal differences.

STANDARDS 1: 2.d., 2: 2.a., 3: 2.d.

Spin a Yarn

How could you make a sweater that will last for 100 years? You would use yarn made from the hair, or fibers, of an alpaca.

Alpaca fibers are shiny, soft, and fine. This makes the fibers easy to spin into yarn. Alpaca yarn is lighter and stronger than yarn made from sheep's wool.

Most alpacas live in South America. Some live in the United States.

 STANDARDS

2.d. *Students know* there is variation among individuals of one kind within a population.

READING

Alpaca yarn is made from alpaca fibers of different colors.

Alpaca fibers come in more colors than any other animal fibers. There are more than 22 colors, even dark red! Breeders choose alpacas for their colors. So when these alpacas reproduce, the offspring may be the colors the breeders like. Some offspring may be different colors. Then there can be more colors of yarn.

Sharing Ideas

1. **Write About It** Make a list of traits that breeders might want in alpaca fibers.

2. **Talk About It** How is knowing about inherited traits helpful to alpaca breeders?

Math Model Division

The picture shows the babies that Jim's hamster had. Jim gave 2 hamsters to each of his 4 friends. Make a drawing to show the groups. How many hamsters did Jim have left for himself?

Writing Describe a Life Cycle

Think about what happens in each stage of a frog's life cycle. Write an adventure story about a frog's life. Tell it from the frog's point of view. Make a drawing to go with your story.

Dr. Ray Wack

Meet Dr. Ray Wack. He is a veterinarian, or a doctor who takes care of animals. He works at the Sacramento Zoo. He cares for many kinds of animals.

Zoo animals are not pets. They come from wild places around the world. Dr. Wack hopes that everyone will protect the wild places where animals live.

This baby animal was born at a zoo. A veterinarian helps take care of it.

Visual Summary

Animals are much like other animals of the same kind. But in some ways they are different.

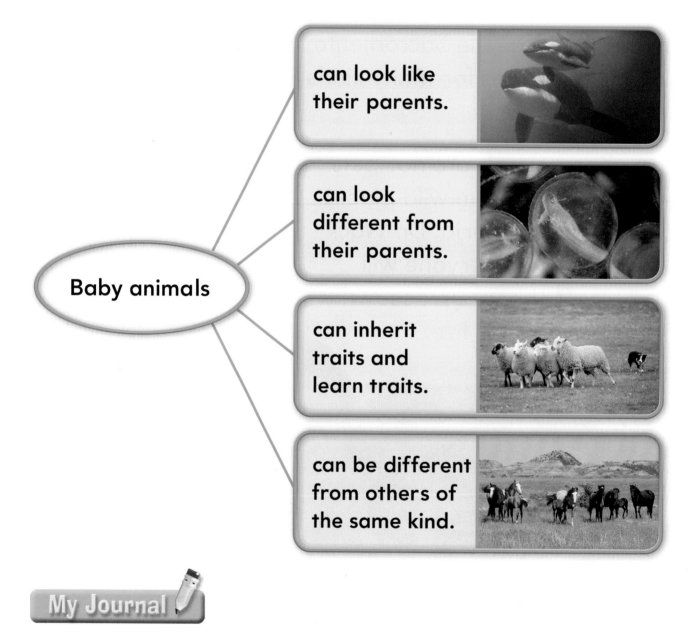

Baby animals

can look like their parents.

can look different from their parents.

can inherit traits and learn traits.

can be different from others of the same kind.

My Journal

Review your answers to the Lesson Preview questions.

STANDARDS 2.a., 2.b., 2.c., 2.d.

Main Ideas

1. How are the life cycles of a bird and a mouse alike and different? (p. 50)

2. Where do animals get their inherited traits? (p. 60)

3. How can animals of the same kind be different? (p. 68)

Vocabulary

Choose the correct word from the box.

4. One living thing in a group of the same kind of living things

5. The living things that come from a living thing

6. To make more living things of the same kind

7. The stage when an insect changes form

reproduce (p. 48)
offspring (p. 48)
pupa (p. 56)
individual (p. 69)

Using Science Skills

8. You find a larva on a leaf. How do you think it will change over time?

9. **Critical Thinking** What is a trait that you inherited? What is a trait that you learned?

STANDARDS 1: 2.b., 2: 2.c., 3–4: 2.d., 5–6: 2.a., 7: 2.b., 8: 2.b., 4.a., 4.d., 9: 2.c.

77

Test Practice

Choose the correct answer.

1. In which plant part do seeds form?

○   ○   ○

2. What might cause one plant to grow tall and one to die?

gravity   fruit   environment

○   ○   ○

3. What is the stage that comes next after this stage?

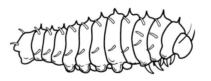

egg   adult   pupa

○   ○   ○

4. What do baby birds look most like?

eggs   baby mice   their parents

○   ○   ○

5. The roots of a plant grow down toward the pull of _____.

light   gravity   soil

○   ○   ○

Checking Main Ideas

Write the correct answer.

6. Describe a plant or animal's life cycle.

7. How can individuals in a population be different?

STANDARDS 1: 2.f., 2: 2.c., 3: 2.b., 4: 2.a., 5: 2.e., 6: 2.b., 7: 2.d.

79

You Can...

Discover More

How do mother sea lions find their pups?

To find their pups, mother sea lions make a loud trumpet sound. Each mother's sound is different. When the pup hears the sound, it makes a bleating sound back. Mother and pup continue until they find each other. The mother knows for sure which pup is hers by its smell.

Simulations Go to **www.eduplace.com/cascp** to learn how animals find their babies.

EARTH [UNIT B] SCIENCE

Earth's Resources

RED ROCK CANYON

Red Rock Canyon was shaped over thousands of years by wind and rainfall.

Beavertail cactuses grow best on dry, rocky, desert slopes in bright sunlight.

The chuckwalla lizard sleeps for seven months out of the year.

Earth's Resources

Reading in Science 82

Chapter 3
Rocks, Soils, and Fossils 84

Independent Books
- Rocks, Soils, and Fossils
- Jack Horner, Dinosaur Hunter
- A Worm's Home

Chapter 4
Using Resources 126

Independent Books
- Using Resources
- It Must Be Clay
- Famous Rocks

Kings Canyon National Park

Earth is made of materials that have distinct properties and provide resources for human activities.

Rocks, Soil, and Fossils

Our Earth is full of treasures

Like minerals and rocks.

Rich soil for growing

And fossils for knowing

The treasures of our Earth.

The treasures of our Earth.

from *Science Songs*, track 12

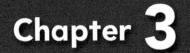

Rocks, Soils, and Fossils

The Grand Canyon

LESSON 1

Rocks are different colors. What are some other ways that rocks are different?

LESSON 2

There are many sizes of rocks. Where do small rocks come from?

LESSON 3

Soil is made of many small parts. What things can you find in soil?

LESSON 4

The animal that made this fossil lived long ago. What can we learn from fossils?

My Journal

Write or draw in your journal to answer the questions above.

Vocabulary

rock p. 90

mineral p. 90

weathering p. 98

erosion p. 100

gravity p. 100

soil p. 104

humus p. 104

nutrients p. 104

fossil p. 114

Picture Glossary

English-Spanish p. H18

Vocabulary Skill

Use Syllables

mineral

Break the word into syllables. Say each syllable aloud, clapping once for each syllable.

rock
A rock is a solid made of one or more minerals.

soil
Soil is the loose material that covers Earth's surface.

fossil
A fossil is something that remains of a living thing from long ago.

weathering

Weathering is the wearing away and breaking apart of rock.

Start with Your Standards

Standard Set 3. Earth Sciences

3.a. *Students know* how to compare the physical properties of different kinds of rocks and know that rock is composed of different combinations of minerals.

3.b. *Students know* smaller rocks come from the breakage and weathering of larger rocks.

3.c. *Students know* that soil is made partly from weathered rock and partly from organic materials and that soils differ in their color, texture, capacity to retain water, and ability to support the growth of many kinds of plants.

3.d. *Students know* that fossils provide evidence about the plants and animals that lived long ago and that scientists learn about the past history of Earth by studying fossils.

Standard Set 4. Investigation and Experimentation covered in this chapter: 4.c., 4.f.

What Makes Up Rocks?

Building Background

Rocks are made up of different kinds of minerals. Different rocks and minerals have different properties.

Inquiry Skill

Measure Use tools and metric units to find weight.

STANDARDS

3.a. *Students know* how to compare the physical properties of different kinds of rocks and know that rock is composed of different combinations of minerals.
4.c. Compare and sort common objects according to two or more physical attributes (e.g., color, shape, texture, size, weight).

rocks and minerals

hand lens and crayons

recording chart

balance

Compare Rocks

Steps

STEP 1

1. **Compare** Look at the rocks. Record their color, texture, and mass.

2. **Work Together** Look at the minerals. Then look closely at each rock again. Compare each rock to the minerals. Share ideas about what you see in each rock.

STEP 2

3. **Classify** Sort the rocks into groups that are alike in two ways. Record your groups. Tell the sorting rule.

STEP 3

Think and Share

1. **Compare** How are rocks different? How are minerals different?

2. **Infer** What did you find in the rocks? How are rocks alike?

Guided Inquiry

Experiment Use a balance to **measure** the mass of some other rocks. Are the biggest samples always the heaviest?

rock

mineral

◎ **Reading Skill**
Classify

Group	Group

STANDARDS

3.a. *Students know* how to compare the physical properties of different kinds of rocks and know that rock is composed of different combinations of minerals.

Red Rock Canyon is made of layers of sandstone.

Rocks and Minerals

When you look at the surface of Earth, you see land and water. Part of the land is rock and part is soil. Underneath the soil and water is rock.

Earth is made up mostly of hard, solid materials called rocks. A **rock** is a solid made of one or more minerals. A **mineral** is a solid found in nature that was never living. Minerals join in different ways to form different kinds of rocks.

Morro Rock is part of an old volcano.

Rocks and minerals are not found only under soil and water. The mountains that line the California coast are made of many different kinds of rocks. The rocks in the canyons of the desert are made up of many smaller rocks.

🎯 **Classify** How can you tell a rock from a mineral?

Express Lab

Activity Card 9
Group Rocks

Properties of Minerals

There are many kinds of minerals. Different minerals have different properties. You can identify minerals by their properties.

One property is hardness. Some minerals, such as diamonds, are very hard. Others, such as talc, are so soft you can scratch them with your fingernail.

turquoise

amethyst in a geode

cinnabar

gypsum

Another property is luster. Luster means how shiny something is. Some minerals are shiny. Other minerals are dull.

A third property is color. Some colorful minerals are used to make jewelry. Some minerals come in different colors.

⊚ Classify What properties can be used to sort minerals?

ruby

opal

emerald

zincite

Properties of Rocks

A rock can be made of one mineral or many minerals. The color of a rock depends on the minerals it contains. Like minerals, rocks may be hard or soft. Granite is a hard rock. Different rocks feel different. Obsidian has a smooth texture. Sandstone feels rough and grainy.

The pieces that make up rocks are different sizes. Conglomerate is made up of large pieces of other rocks. Limestone is made up of very tiny mineral pieces.

🎯 **Classify** **How can you sort rocks?**

sandstone

limestone

obsidian

conglomerate

Minerals in Rock

Granite is a rock made up of the minerals quartz, feldspar, and mica.

Quartz can be clear or gray.

Feldspar is found in many rocks.

Mica is made of shiny layers.

Lesson Wrap-Up

❶ **Vocabulary** What is a **rock**?

❷ ◎**Reading Skill** How can you tell whether two rocks are made of the same minerals?

❸ **Measure** How can measuring help you compare rocks?

📷 **Technology** Visit www.eduplace.com/cascp to find out more about rocks and minerals.

STANDARDS 1–2: 3.a., 3: 4.b.

How Do Rocks Change?

Building Background

Small rocks are pieces that have broken off larger rocks. Wind and water can wear away large rocks and make them smaller, too.

Inquiry Skill

Infer Instead of guessing, use what you observe and know to tell what you think.

STANDARDS

3.b. *Students know* smaller rocks come from the breakage and weathering of larger rocks.
4.f. Use magnifiers or microscopes to observe and draw descriptions of small objects or small features of objects.

What You Need

goggles

jar with lid and water

rocks

hand lens

Changing Rocks

Steps

STEP 1

1. Put some rocks in a jar. Fill the jar halfway with water. Tightly seal the jar with a lid. **Safety:** Wear goggles!

STEP 2

2. Have each person in your group shake the jar 50 times.

3. **Observe** Put the jar on a table. Leave the jar for 5 minutes. Use a hand lens to look for changes inside the jar.

STEP 3

Think and Share

1. **Communicate** Write or draw steps describing how the rocks changed.

2. **Infer** Where do small pieces of rock come from?

Guided Inquiry

Experiment What other ways can you make small rocks from bigger rocks? Try one way. **Observe** what happens.

Vocabulary

weathering

erosion

gravity

⊙ Reading Skill
Cause and Effect

Cause	→	Effect

STANDARDS

3.b. *Students know* smaller rocks come from the breakage and weathering of larger rocks.

Weathering

Weathering is the wearing away and breaking apart of rock. Rock breaks into smaller and smaller pieces. Then the little bits of rock can become part of soil.

Wind, water, and plants can cause weathering. Water gets into the cracks in rock. The water freezes and thaws over and over. The cracks get bigger. Then the rock breaks into smaller pieces.

⊙ Cause and Effect What are three causes of weathering?

Wind and water together caused parts of these rocks to wear away.

Express Lab

Activity Card 10
Observe How Rocks Change

This rock was broken apart by water freezing and thawing many times.

Water moved across these rocks. Their edges are now rounded.

Roots grew into cracks in this rock. The roots split the rock into pieces.

Erosion

Another change to Earth's surface is erosion. **Erosion** is the carrying of weathered rock and soil from place to place. Water, wind, and gravity can cause erosion. **Gravity** is a force that pulls all objects toward each other.

Gravity causes water to run downhill. Water moving downhill in a river can move rocks and soil. Frozen water in the form of a glacier can slowly move rock and soil down a mountain.

Cause and Effect What causes erosion?

The dark stripes are rock and soil that the glacier picked up as it moved.

Ocean waves crash onto the shore. Some land is pulled away as the waves move back to the ocean.

Strong gusts of wind pick up sandy soil and move it to new places.

Lesson Wrap-Up

❶ Vocabulary What is **erosion**?

❷ 🎯 Reading Skill How can plants cause weathering?

❸ Infer What can you infer about this rock from its shape?

🖳 **Technology** Visit www.eduplace.com/cascp to find out more about weathering.

What Makes Up Soil?

Building Background

Soil is made from bits of rock and rotting materials. Different soils have different properties. Plants grow in soil.

Inquiry Skill

Compare You can compare objects by two or more properties.

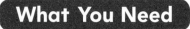

goggles

hand lens

soil samples

STANDARDS

3.c. *Students know* that soil is made partly from weathered rock and partly from organic materials and that soils differ in their color, texture, capacity to retain water, and ability to support the growth of many kinds of plants.
4.c. Compare and sort common objects according to two or more physical attributes (e.g., color, shape, texture, size, weight).

Compare Soils

Steps

1. **Observe** Touch each soil sample. Rub a bit between your fingers. **Safety:** Wear goggles!

STEP 1

2. **Observe** Use a hand lens. Look at each soil sample. Notice the color and the materials that are in it. **Safety:** Wash your hands!

STEP 2

3. **Record Data** Draw what each sample looks like under the hand lens.

4. **Classify** Sort the soil samples. The soils in each group should be alike in two ways.

STEP 3

Think and Share

1. **Compare** How are the soils alike and different?

2. **Infer** Why do you think the soils are different colors?

Guided Inquiry

Experiment Talk with others about how to find out more about the soil where you live. Choose a plan to follow. **Communicate** to the group what to do.

Vocabulary

soil

humus

nutrients

◎ **Reading Skill**

Compare and Contrast

Different	Alike	Different

▚ **STANDARDS**

3.c. *Students know* that soil is made partly from weathered rock and partly from organic materials and that soils differ in their color, texture, capacity to retain water, and ability to support the growth of many kinds of plants.

How Soil Is Made

Soil is the loose material that covers Earth's surface. Soil contains bits of weathered rock, humus, air, and water.

Humus is tiny bits of dead plants and animals in soil. Humus contains nutrients. **Nutrients** are materials that help a plant grow well.

How Humus Forms

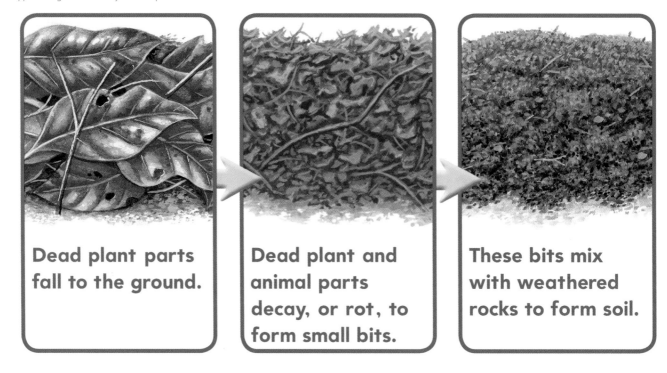

Dead plant parts fall to the ground.

Dead plant and animal parts decay, or rot, to form small bits.

These bits mix with weathered rocks to form soil.

Soil forms in layers. Humus forms in the top layer. The next layer has small pieces of weathered rock. The bottom layer is made of large, broken rocks. Over a long time, these rocks can weather to become the small rock and mineral parts of soil.

Compare and Contrast How are the three layers of soil different?

Layers of Soil

Top Layer
This layer is rich in humus. Plants grow here.

Middle Layer
This layer has less humus. Small rocks collect here.

Bottom Layer
Tree roots can grow down into this layer of larger rocks.

How Soils Differ

Different soils have different properties. They have different amounts of weathered rock, humus, air, and water.

Soils that have a lot of humus are often dark in color. Other soils are made up mostly of weathered rock and minerals with iron. These soils are usually red. Some soils feel gritty, and others are sticky. Some soils hold a great deal of water. Others hold very little.

Compare and Contrast How are soils different?

Dark soil is good for growing many plants.

Express Lab

Activity Card 11
Compare Soils

Kinds of Soil

Topsoil	Clay Soil	Sandy Soil
• has a lot of humus • is dark in color • is best for plant growth	• is made of tiny clay pieces • is sticky when wet • is brown, red, or yellow	• has a lot of weathered rock • feels gritty • is tan or light brown

Animals Help Soil

Many animals live in soil. Some animals dig in soil. Others move through the soil. Animals loosen the soil by breaking it into smaller pieces. Air can enter the soil between the smaller pieces.

When it rains, water can soak into the soil instead of running over the surface. This keeps soil from washing away.

wood lice

earthworm

Earthworms eat bits of soil as they move through it. Wood lice eat rotting plants and break them down into smaller bits.

Gophers make long tunnels through the soil. They mix the soil as they dig. They push the soil from the tunnels toward the surface. This helps plant roots reach the nutrients they need more easily.

Gophers burrow in soil. Their tunnels help air and water move through soil.

◎ Compare and Contrast How do different animals help soil?

Lesson Wrap-Up

❶ **Vocabulary** Where do plants get **nutrients**?

❷ ◎**Reading Skill** What are three ways in which soils differ?

❸ **Compare** What makes topsoil different from sandy soil?

📖 **Technology** Visit **www.eduplace.com/cascp** to find out more about soil.

STANDARDS 1–3: 3.c.

EXTREME Science

Mighty MITE

Is it a giant beast from another planet? No. It is just an extreme close-up picture of a soil mite. Most mites are smaller than the period at the end of this sentence.

Soil mites help break down dead plants and animals to make humus. This process adds nutrients to the soil and helps plants grow.

The soil this girl is holding probably has 50 thousand mites in it!

This picture of a soil mite was taken through a powerful microscope.

My Journal

How do soil mites help make better soil? Write your ideas in your journal.

What Clues Do Fossils Give?

Building Background

Fossils give clues about plants and animals that lived long ago. Different fossils give different clues.

Inquiry Skill

Classify You can sort a group of objects by two or more properties.

What You Need

fossils

hand lens

ruler

 STANDARDS

3.d. *Students know* that fossils provide evidence about the plants and animals that lived long ago and that scientists learn about the past history of Earth by studying fossils.
4.c. Compare and sort common objects according to two or more physical attributes (e.g., color, shape, texture, size, weight).

Compare Fossils

Steps

STEP 1

① **Observe** Look at each fossil. Draw what you see. Then use a hand lens to look at each fossil again. Add details to your drawings.

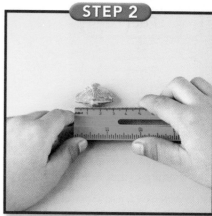

STEP 2

② **Measure** Use a ruler. Measure the length of each fossil in centimeters. Add this data to your drawings.

STEP 3

③ **Classify** Sort the fossils into groups. The fossils in each group should be alike in two ways.

④ **Communicate** Talk about what living things the fossils look like.

Think and Share

1. How could you tell which fossils were animals and which ones were plants?

2. **Infer** What might a scientist learn by comparing fossil leaves to leaves of plants today?

Guided Inquiry

Ask Questions Make a list of questions about the fossils you have seen. Communicate with classmates about how to find answers.

▶ **Vocabulary**

fossil

◎ **Reading Skill**
**Draw
Conclusions**

Fact

↓

Fact

↓

Conclusion

STANDARDS

3.d. *Students know* that fossils provide
evidence about the plants and animals that
lived long ago and that scientists learn about
the past history of Earth by studying fossils.

How Fossils Form

People learn about once-living things by studying fossils. A **fossil** is something that remains of a living thing from long ago. Fossils form in different ways.

Some fossils are imprints. When a living thing presses down in soft mud, it leaves a shape in the mud. Over time, the mud turns to rock. The shape of a living thing found in rock is an imprint.

How Casts Form

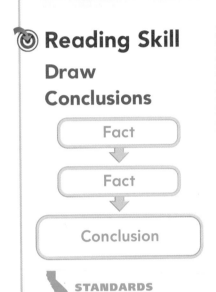

1 A living thing dies and is buried in mud. The mud turns to rock.

2 The hard part of the living thing breaks down. Its imprint is left in rock.

Some fossils are hard parts of animals, such as bones or teeth. After the animals died, layers of mud covered them. The soft parts of the animals rotted away. Over millions of years, the hard parts turned to rock. These are some of the fossils that people find and study today.

fossil bone

Draw Conclusions What can you conclude from finding a fossil in rock?

leaf imprint

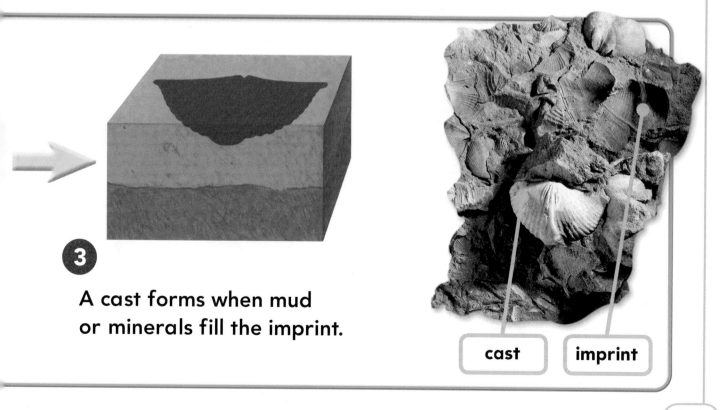

3

A cast forms when mud or minerals fill the imprint.

cast   imprint

Learning from Fossils

Fossils give clues about plants and animals that lived long ago. Some of those plants and animals, such as dinosaurs, no longer live on Earth.

Fossil bones give clues about the size of an animal. Imprints and casts give clues about how a plant or an animal looked. Tracks show how an animal moved.

Draw Conclusions What would a long, thick leg bone tell you about an animal?

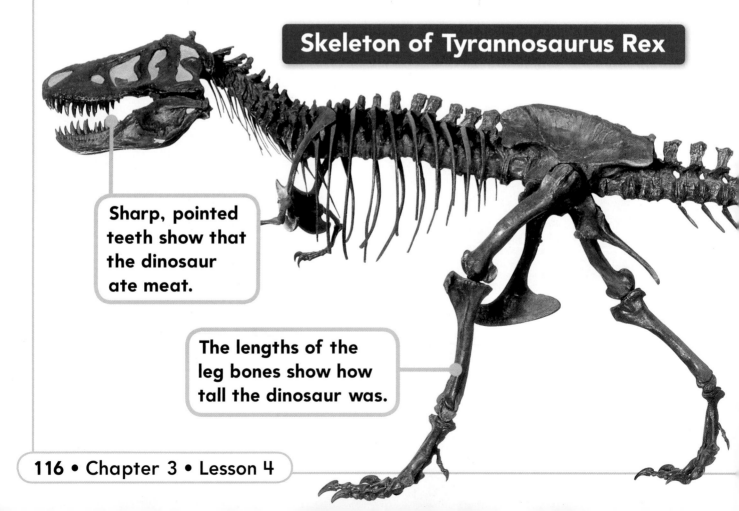

Skeleton of Tyrannosaurus Rex

Sharp, pointed teeth show that the dinosaur ate meat.

The lengths of the leg bones show how tall the dinosaur was.

What clues might an artist use to draw a picture of a dinosaur?

Footprints give clues about the weight and speed of the dinosaur.

Express Lab

Activity Card 12
Group Fossils

Clues to Earth's Past

Many plants and animals living today are like those that lived long ago. People study fossils to see how living things have changed over time. Scientists look at the bones of dinosaurs and compare them with bones of animals living today. This has led some scientists to think that birds are related to some dinosaurs.

Ferns once formed huge forests. Today most ferns grow on forest floors.

fossil fern imprint

Long Ago

Now

The land where these fossils were found was probably once under water.

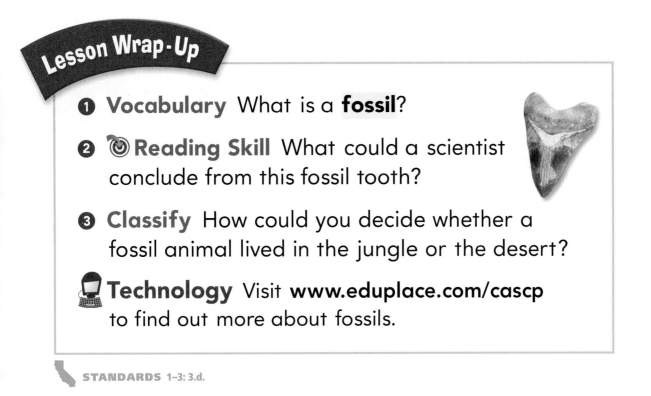

Scientists also look for clues about environments of long ago. They compare fossils to living things. Then they infer what the environment might have been.

Draw Conclusions What can you learn about plant fossils by comparing them to plants today?

Lesson Wrap-Up

❶ **Vocabulary** What is a **fossil**?

❷ **Reading Skill** What could a scientist conclude from this fossil tooth?

❸ **Classify** How could you decide whether a fossil animal lived in the jungle or the desert?

Technology Visit **www.eduplace.com/cascp** to find out more about fossils.

STANDARDS 1–3: 3.d.

Fossils of Saber-Toothed Cats

Many saber-toothed cat fossils have been found at Rancho La Brea in Los Angeles. Rancho La Brea is also called the Tar Pits.

At first, scientists thought the cats used their huge teeth to grab and hold prey. The teeth would have broken. But few broken teeth have been found. Now scientists believe that saber-toothed cats used their large teeth to stab prey.

This is a skull of a saber-toothed cat, California's state fossil.

STANDARDS

3.d. *Students know* that fossils provide evidence about the plants and animals that lived long ago and that scientists learn about the past history of Earth by studying fossils.

READING **LINK**

Pit 91 is the only pit at La Brea in which people still search for fossils each summer.

Sharing Ideas

1. **Write About It** How have ideas about a saber-toothed cat's teeth changed over time?

2. **Talk About It** Why might scientists change their ideas about animals of the past?

121

Math Measure Dinosaur Footprints

Use a ruler. Measure the dinosaur footprint in inches. Record your measurement. Predict whether measuring in centimeters will give you a larger or smaller number. Measure the footprint in centimeters to find out.

Writing Describe How a Fossil Forms

Suppose that you can watch a clam shell change into a cast fossil over time. Write the steps. Tell what happens at each step. Tell what the fossil looks like when it is found.

Geologist

Do you like to learn about Earth? If so, you might like to be a geologist. Geologists study Earth's air, land, and water. They also study the layers of Earth below the surface. Some geologists look for useful Earth resources, such as coal, oil, and iron.

What It Takes!

- A college degree in geology or Earth science
- Skills in math and in reading maps

Review and Practice

Visual Summary

Different rocks, minerals, and soils can be found on Earth. Scientists study fossils to learn about living things from long ago.

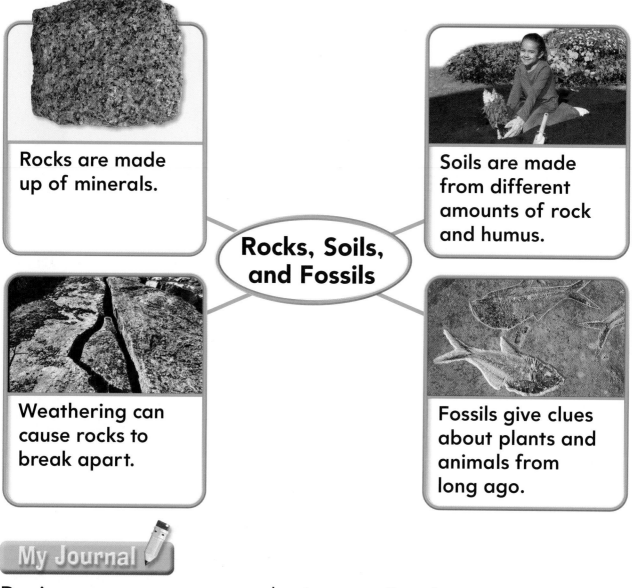

Rocks are made up of minerals.

Soils are made from different amounts of rock and humus.

Weathering can cause rocks to break apart.

Rocks, Soils, and Fossils

Fossils give clues about plants and animals from long ago.

My Journal

Review your answers to the Lesson Preview questions.

STANDARDS 3.a., 3.b., 3.c., 3.d.

Main Ideas

1. What are rocks made of? (p. 90)

2. How is soil with a lot of humus different from other soils? (pp. 106–107)

3. What can scientists learn from fossils? (p. 116)

Vocabulary

Choose the correct word from the box.

4. The wearing away and breaking apart of rock

5. Materials that help a plant grow well

6. The carrying of weathered rock and soil from place to place

7. A force that pulls all objects toward each other

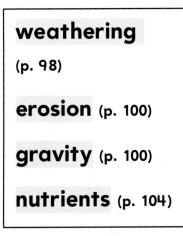

weathering
(p. 98)

erosion (p. 100)

gravity (p. 100)

nutrients (p. 104)

Using Science Skills

8. How can you sort rocks into groups so that the rocks in each group are alike in two ways?

9. **Critical Thinking** Where do you think small pieces of rock on a hiking path come from?

STANDARDS 1: 3.a., 2: 3.c., 3: 3.d., 4: 3.b., 5: 3.c., 6–7: 3.b., 8: 4.c., 3.a., 9: 3.b.

Chapter 4

Using Resources

Middle McCloud Falls in Northern California

LESSON 1

This wall is made of rock. What are some other uses of rocks?

LESSON 2

Water is a resource. What are some ways people use water?

LESSON 3

Plants grow in soil. What are some uses of plants and soil?

LESSON 4

You can recycle to save resources. How else can people save resources?

ONLY

My Journal

Write or draw in your journal to answer the questions above.

Vocabulary Preview

Vocabulary

natural resource p. 132

fuel p. 132

irrigation p. 144

fertile p. 148

conserve p. 156

recycle p. 158

Picture Glossary

English-Spanish p. H18

Vocabulary Skill

Use Pictures

irrigation

Say the word aloud. Use clues from the picture to help you understand what the word means.

natural resource

A natural resource is something found in nature that people need or use.

conserve

When you conserve, you use less of something to make it last longer.

recycle

When you recycle, you collect used materials to make new items.

irrigation

Irrigation is a way to bring water to dry land.

Start with Your Standards

Standard Set 3. Earth Sciences

3.a. *Students know* how to compare the physical properties of different kinds of rocks and know that rock is composed of different combinations of minerals.

3.c. *Students know* that soil is made partly from weathered rock and partly from organic materials and that soils differ in their color, texture, capacity to retain water, and ability to support the growth of many kinds of plants.

3.e. *Students know* rock, water, plants, and soil provide many resources, including food, fuel, and building materials, that humans use.

Standard Set 4. Investigation and Experimentation covered in this chapter: 4.b., 4.e., 4.f.

How Do People Use Rocks?

Building Background

Rocks are used in many ways. They are used in buildings, statues, jewelry, and glass.

Inquiry Skill

Communicate Share with others what you learn and observe.

What You Need

paper and crayons

hand lens

STANDARDS

3.e. *Students know* rock, water, plants, and soil provide many resources, including food, fuel, and building materials, that humans use.
4.f. Use magnifiers or microscopes to observe and draw descriptions of small objects or small features of objects.

Look for Rocks

Steps

STEP 1

1 **Observe** Take a walk around the school. Walk both inside and outside. Look for things made of rocks. Draw what you see.

STEP 2

2 **Observe** Use a hand lens to look closely at things made of rocks. Add the details you see to your drawings.

3 **Communicate** Compare your drawings with those of a partner. Talk about the ways that people use rocks.

STEP 3

Think and Share

1. **Compare** How are objects made of rock different?

2. **Infer** Why do you think people use rocks in these different ways?

Guided Inquiry

Ask Questions Take a class survey. Find out how many children live in homes made with rocks or without rocks. **Use data** to make a bar graph of your results.

► **Vocabulary**

natural resource
fuel

⊙ **Reading Skill**
**Main Idea
and Details**

Main
Idea

◤ **STANDARDS**

3.e. *Students know* rock, water, plants, and
soil provide many resources, including food,
fuel, and building materials, that humans use.
3.a. *Students know* how to compare the
physical properties of different kinds of rocks
and know that rock is composed of different
combinations of minerals.

**The same rock bits
that make up sand
on a beach in
Carmel are used for
building materials.**

Express Lab

Activity Card 13
Identify Rock Uses

Resources from Rocks

A **natural resource** is something found in nature that people need or use. Rocks, water, and soil are some natural resources.

Rocks are used for building materials and fuel. A **fuel** is a material that is burned to provide power or heat. Coal is a rock that is used for fuel. It is burned to make heat. Sand is made up of bits of weathered rock. It can be mixed with other materials to make sidewalks and some buildings.

⊙ **Main Idea** What are rocks used for?

Ways People Use Rocks

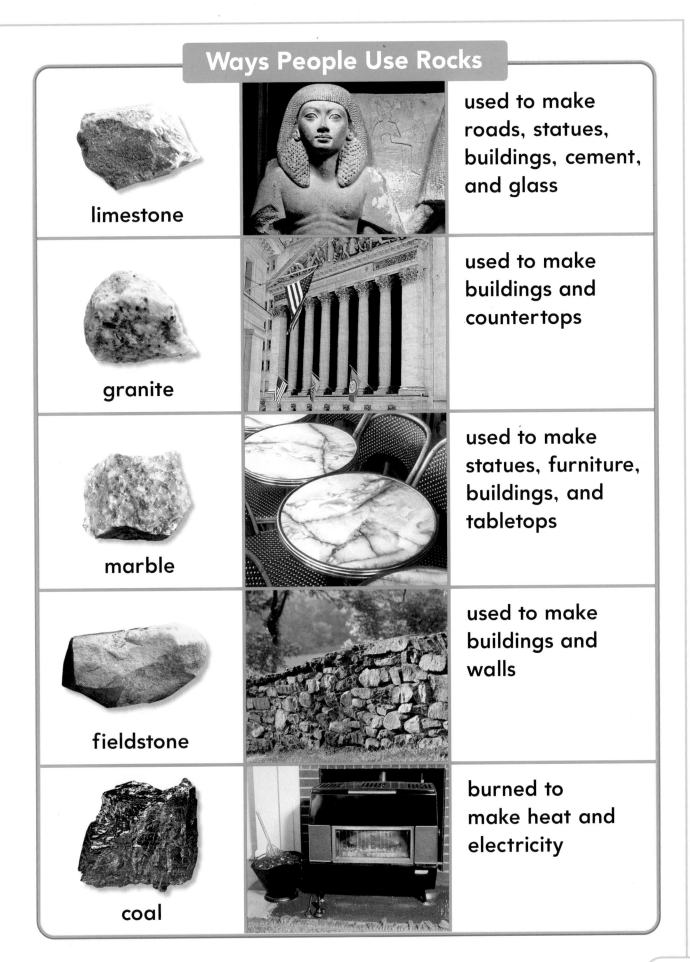

limestone		used to make roads, statues, buildings, cement, and glass
marble		used to make statues, furniture, buildings, and tabletops
fieldstone		used to make buildings and walls
coal		burned to make heat and electricity

granite — used to make buildings and countertops

Uses of Minerals

The minerals in rocks are used to make many things. Gold and copper are used to make coins, metals, and jewelry. Garnet and diamond are used to make jewelry, too. Graphite is softer than garnet. It is used in pencils. Because talc is so soft, it is used in powder.

Main Idea What are some ways in which the minerals in rocks are used?

garnet

graphite

gold

talc

Quartz is used in the parts that make a watch run. Quartz is also used in the glass of some watches.

quartz

Lesson Wrap-Up

❶ **Vocabulary** What is a **natural resource**?

❷ 🎯 **Reading Skill** What are three ways in which rocks and minerals are used?

❸ **Communicate** Why are rocks and minerals important natural resources?

💻 **Technology** Visit **www.eduplace.com/cascp** to find out more about rocks and minerals that are found in California.

STANDARDS 1: 3.e., 2: 3.a., 3.e., 3: 3.e.

Rock Stars

Cast

Narrator

Paul: a sculptor

Susan: a jeweler

Art: a builder

Jon: a road worker

Carla: a miner

STANDARDS

3.e. *Students know* rock, water, plants, and soil provide many resources, including food, fuel, and building materials, that humans use.

READING **LINK**

Narrator: People use rocks in many ways. Some jobs depend on rocks.

Paul: I am a sculptor. I carve rocks to make art.

Carla: What kind of rocks do you use?

Paul: I use marble. Marble is a pretty rock. It is very strong, too.

Art: I am a builder. I use rocks that are hard and pretty, too! I like sandstone and granite.

Susan: What do you use them for?

Art: I cut and polish rocks to make blocks and tiles. I use the blocks and tiles in buildings.

Susan: I am a jeweler. I cut and polish pretty rocks, too. I use them to make jewelry.

Jon: I am a road worker. I use crushed rocks, like limestone, to make concrete to build roads.

Carla: Very interesting. But you would not have jobs without me!

Paul, Susan, Art, and Jon: Why?

Carla: I am a miner. I dig up rocks from the ground. Then people like you can use them!

Paul, Susan, Art, and Jon: Thanks Carla! You rock!

Sharing Ideas

1. **Write About It** Why do you think different rocks are used for different jobs?

2. **Talk About It** What would your life be like without rocks?

How Do People Use Water?

Building Background

People use water in many ways. They use it for drinking, watering plants, washing, and having fun.

Inquiry Skill

Record Data You can make and label a bar graph to record data.

paper and pencil

bar graph

STANDARDS

3.e. *Students know* rock, water, plants, and soil provide many resources, including food, fuel, and building materials, that humans use.
4.e. Construct bar graphs to record data, using appropriately labeled axes.

Water Use

Steps

1 **Record Data** Keep track of how many times you use water during one school day. Use a tally chart like the one shown.

2 **Use Numbers** Work with a group. Count the total number of tally marks for each way that water was used.

3 **Record Data** Use the group totals to make a bar graph of your group's water use.

Ways I Used Water	Tally
Drinking	
Washing Hands	
Flushing Toilet	
Washing Objects	

Think and Share

1. **Use Data** How was water used most often by your group? How was water used least?

2. How would your graph change if you collected data for the whole class?

Guided Inquiry

Ask Questions How would your graph change if you collected data for _____? **Predict** how water would be used most.

141

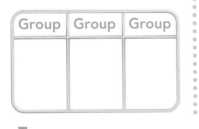
▶ **Vocabulary**

irrigation

◎ **Reading Skill**
Classify

Group	Group	Group

STANDARDS

3.e. *Students know* rock, water, plants, and soil provide many resources, including food, fuel, and building materials, that humans use.

People Use Water

Water is a natural resource that you cannot live without. All living things need water to live and grow. Without water, living things would die.

You use water every day in many ways. Water is in most things that you drink. It is used to cook many foods that you eat. You use water when you take a bath or brush your teeth.

bathing

drinking

Water is also used to clean many things. Every time you help with the dishes or the laundry, you are using water.

People use water to put out fires. This water comes from lakes, rivers, and oceans. The water that you drink and bathe in comes from lakes, rivers, and under the ground.

having fun

🎯 **Classify** **What are three ways in which people use water at home?**

washing hands

fighting fires

Express Lab

Activity Card 14
Categorize Water Uses

Water for Farming

Like all living things, plants need water to live and grow. In some places, it rains often. Plants get the water they need.

Some places do not get enough rain. Then farmers have to find another way to water their crops. **Irrigation** is a way to bring water to dry land. Ditches and pipes are used to carry water from streams, rivers, and wells to the farms.

Many farmers in California use irrigation to bring water to their crops.

Water for Electricity

Water moving through a dam is used to power machines that make electricity. The Hoover Dam provides electricity for parts of California, Nevada, and Arizona. The dam makes enough electricity for more than a million people to use each day.

Hoover Dam

Classify What are two ways in which crops get water?

Lesson Wrap-Up

❶ **Vocabulary** What is **irrigation**?

❷ **Reading Skill** Where does the water that people use come from?

❸ **Record Data** What are two ways that you can record data?

Technology Visit **www.eduplace.com/cascp** to find out more about how people use water.

STANDARDS 1–3: 3.e.

How Do People Use Soil and Plants?

Building Background

Some soils hold more water than others. Different plants grow in different kinds of soil. Plants can be used for food, fuel, and building materials.

Inquiry Skill

Use Numbers Use numbers to describe and compare objects or events.

STANDARDS

3.c. *Students know* that soil is made partly from weathered rock and partly from organic materials and that soils differ in their color, texture, capacity to retain water, and ability to support the growth of many kinds of plants.
4.e. Construct bar graphs to record data, using appropriately labeled axes.

What You Need

goggles

soils, measuring cup, and water

funnel, filters, and cylinder

bar graph

Water in Soil

Steps

STEP 1

1. Place a filter in a funnel. Place the funnel in a cylinder. Fill the filter halfway with topsoil. **Safety:** Wear goggles!

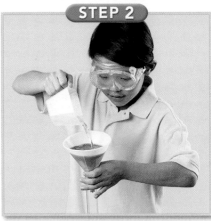

STEP 2

2. **Measure** Fill a measuring cup with 100 milliliters of water. Slowly pour the water onto the soil. Wait one minute.

3. **Use Numbers** Measure how much water collected. Record the data on a graph.

STEP 3

4. Repeat steps 1–3 for the other soils. **Safety:** Wash your hands!

Think and Share

1. **Use Numbers** Compare your data. Through which soil did the most water pass?

2. **Infer** Which soil could you use for a plant that does not need much water? Tell why.

Guided Inquiry

Experiment Plant the same kind of seed in each soil sample. **Observe** the plants for one week. Find out which soil is best for that plant's growth.

147

🔻 **STANDARDS**

3.c. *Students know* that soil is made partly from weathered rock and partly from organic materials and that soils differ in their color, texture, capacity to retain water, and ability to support the growth of many kinds of plants.
3.e. *Students know* rock, water, plants, and soil provide many resources, including food, fuel, and building materials, that humans use.

Plants Need Soil

Plants take in the water and nutrients they need from soil. Soil that is **fertile** is full of the nutrients needed to grow plants. Fertile soil is rich in humus. Humus provides important nutrients to soil. It also helps soil hold water.

Soils have different properties. Some soils, such as clay soil, hold a lot of water. Others, such as sandy soil, do not. A cactus, which stores water in its stem, grows well in sandy soil.

🎯 **Classify** What two things do growing plants need from soil?

To grow well, different plants need soils with different properties.

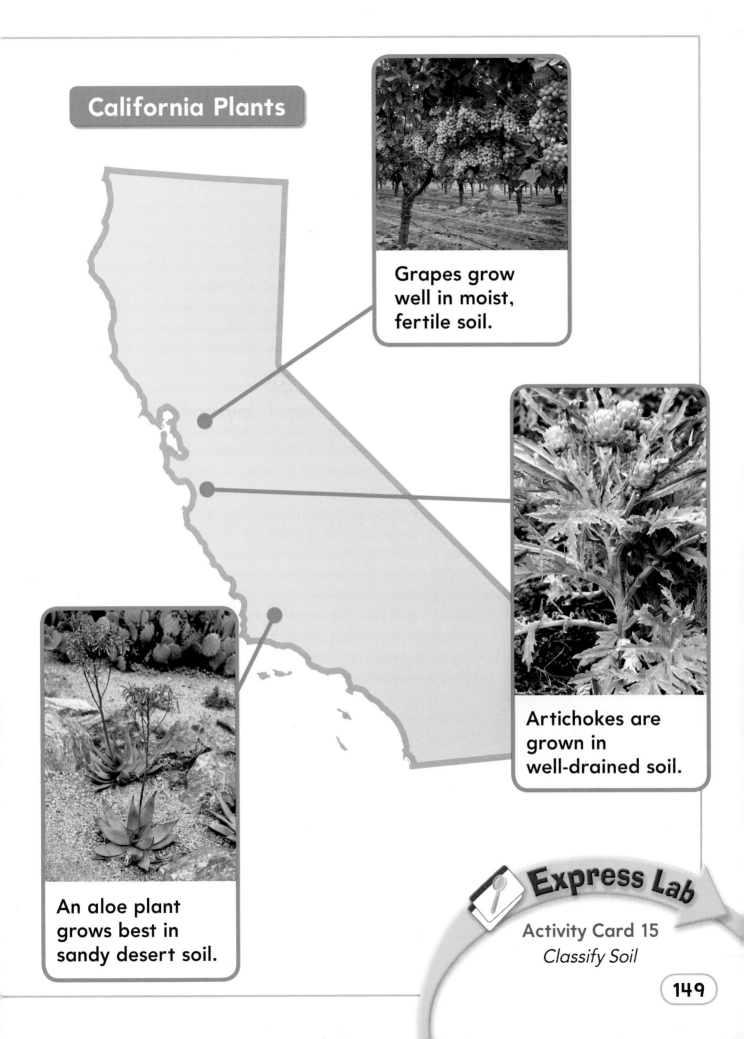

California Plants

Grapes grow well in moist, fertile soil.

Artichokes are grown in well-drained soil.

An aloe plant grows best in sandy desert soil.

Express Lab

Activity Card 15
Classify Soil

Uses of Soil and Trees

Like rocks and water, soil and trees are natural resources. People use soil and trees for many things.

People use soil to grow food for themselves and for animals. Some soils can be used to make building materials. Clay soil can be formed into adobe bricks. Adobe bricks can be found both inside and outside a building. Clay soil can also be used to make roof tiles.

The roof and walls of this home are made from clay.

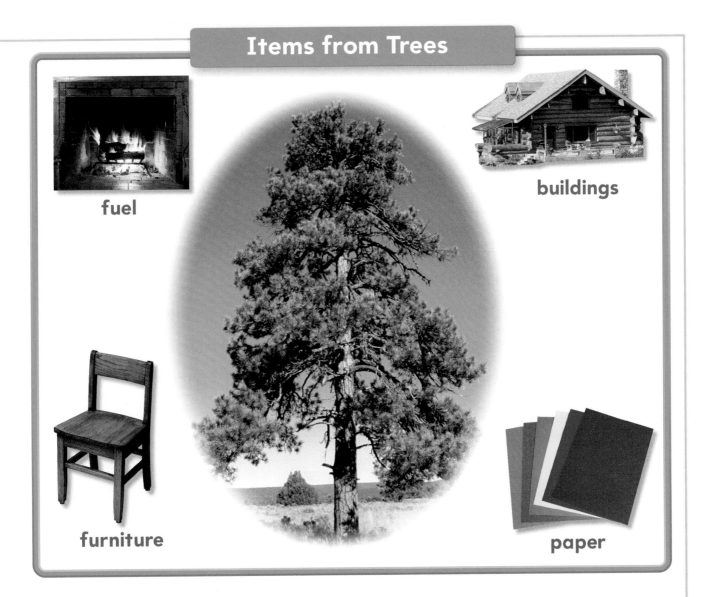

fuel

buildings

furniture

paper

Trees are plants that have many uses. Wood from trees is used to build homes and make furniture. Paper and pencils that you use every day are made from wood.

Wood is also burned to make heat. The heat is used to warm homes and cook food. Some trees also produce fruit. This fruit provides food for people and animals.

Classify Name four items made from trees.

Uses of Plants

Trees are not the only plants that people use. <u>Many items that people use come from different kinds of plants.</u>

Some items made from plants are cardboard, rubber, cork, clothing, furniture, and medicine. Cotton is a plant that is used to make clothing. Bamboo is a plant that is used to make placemats, furniture, and flooring.

cotton

oats

bamboo

strawberries

Chickens eat the seeds of a corn plant.

Plants are a very important source of food for people. Leaves are eaten in salads, and fruits are eaten as snacks. Plants are also used to make foods such as cereals.

Many animals eat plants. Some of the meats that people eat are from animals that eat plants.

Classify **What is a cotton plant used for?**

Lesson Wrap-Up

❶ **Vocabulary** What is **fertile** soil?

❷ **Reading Skill** How are plants used as fuel?

❸ **Use Numbers** How can you use numbers to compare the amount of water soils hold?

Technology Visit **www.eduplace.com/cascp** to find out more about the uses of plants and soil.

STANDARDS 1: 3.c. ; 2–3: 3.e.

How Can People Save Resources?

Building Background

People can help save resources by not wasting them, using less of them, and reusing what they can.

Inquiry Skill

Use Models You can use something like a real thing to find out more about the real thing.

▎STANDARDS

3.e. *Students know* rock, water, plants, and soil provide many resources, including food, fuel, and building materials, that humans use.
4.b. Measure length, weight, temperature, and liquid volume with appropriate tools and express those measurements in standard metric system units.

What You Need

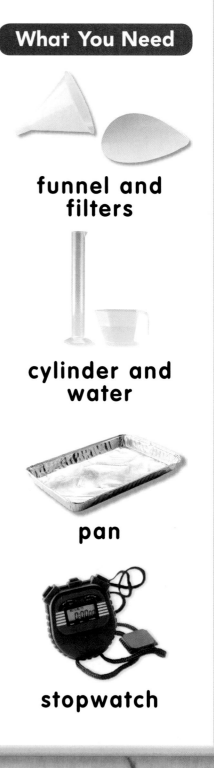

funnel and filters

cylinder and water

pan

stopwatch

Wasted Water

Steps

1. **Use Models** Put four filters in a funnel. Put the funnel in the top of a cylinder. The funnel is a model of a leaky faucet.

STEP 1

2. Stand the cylinder in a pan. Pour some water into the funnel. Wait one minute.

STEP 2

3. **Measure** Remove the funnel. Measure the amount of water in the cylinder. Record the measurement.

STEP 3

Think and Share

1. **Compare** Share your results with a classmate. How were the results alike or different? Tell why.

2. **Predict** How much water would a leaky faucet waste in five minutes?

Guided Inquiry

Experiment Record how much paper your class uses during one day. **Predict** how much paper your class will use during one week. Test your prediction.

▶ **Vocabulary**

conserve

recycle

◎ **Reading Skill**

Draw Conclusions

Fact

⬇

Fact

⬇

Conclusion

STANDARDS

3.e. *Students know* rock, water, plants, and soil provide many resources, including food, fuel, and building materials, that humans use.

Conserving Resources

People can conserve Earth's natural resources. When you **conserve** something, you use less of it to make it last longer. Some resources, such as gas and oil, cannot be replaced after they have been used. That is why people should conserve these resources whenever they can.

People can conserve fuel by riding a bike instead of driving. They can conserve water by fixing leaky faucets.

◎ **Draw Conclusions** What might happen if people use too much oil?

Walk or ride your bike instead of riding in a car.

Express Lab

Activity Card 16
Model Water Waste

156

Conserving at Home

Turn off the water while you brush your teeth.

Turn off lights when you leave a room.

Wash full loads of clothes.

Recycling

Recycling can also help save natural resources. When you **recycle**, you collect items made of materials that can be used again to make new items. People recycle newspapers, paper, plastic, and cans. People also recycle glass, rubber, batteries, and cardboard.

plastic bottles

backpack

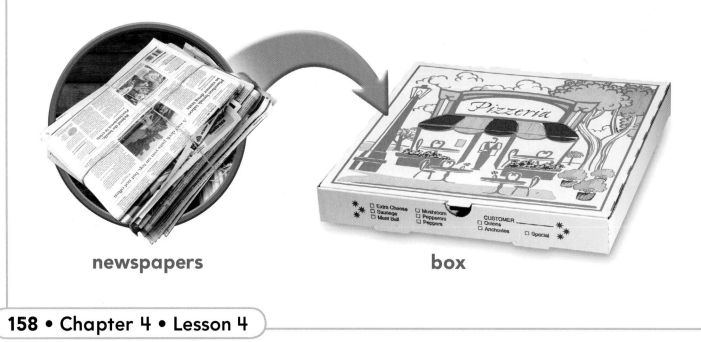

newspapers

box

Recycling newspapers conserves trees. Glass is made from sand. And sand is made up of crushed rocks. So recycling glass conserves rocks and minerals.

Recycling rubber, paper, and cardboard saves plants. Recycling also conserves fuel and water. Less fuel is used to make items from recycled materials than is used to make items from natural resources.

glass

beads

Draw Conclusions What natural resources are you conserving when you recycle newspapers?

Lesson Wrap-Up

❶ **Vocabulary** How do people **recycle**?

❷ **Reading Skill** How does taking a shorter shower help conserve resources?

❸ **Use Models** How can using a model of a leaky faucet help you learn about saving resources?

Technology Visit **www.eduplace.com/cascp** to learn more about conservation.

STANDARDS 1–3: 3.e.

STANDARDS 3.e. *Students know* rock, water, plants, and soil provide many resources, including food, fuel, and building materials, that humans use.

Trash Bird

Would you believe that this huge sculpture is made from trash? The artist found a fun way to reuse objects that most people throw out. Most trash is dumped, burned, or buried. People are now trying to find ways to reuse trash so they can save natural resources.

In 1960, the average American family threw out about 4$\frac{1}{2}$ kilograms of trash each day. By 2000, families were throwing out twice as much.

My Journal

How could you save natural resources by reusing trash? Write or draw your ideas in your journal.

Math Read a Table

For one week, Ms. Sanchez's class collected items to recycle. The table shows how many items they collected.

Kind of Item	Number Collected
plastic bottles	25
cans	17
cardboard boxes	9

1. How many more bottles did the class collect than cans?

2. Which number sentence could be used to find out how many boxes and cans the class collected in one week?

$17 + 9 = \boxed{}$ $17 - 9 = \boxed{}$

Writing Thank-you Letter

Find out who collects items at your local recycling center. Write a thank-you letter to a person who helps conserve natural resources.

October 6, 2007

Dear Mr. Ward,

Thank you for helping us recycle paper. It feels good to know we are saving trees.

Your friend,
Mia

Dr. Randy Dahlgren

Why are some soils different from others? How do plants change soil as they grow? Dr. Randy Dahlgren can answer these questions. Dr. Dahlgren is a soil scientist. He studies soils and plants at the university in Davis, California.

Sometimes soils near factories, highways, and mines can become damaged or polluted. People may ask Dr. Dahlgren to help them fix the soil. He also works with farmers to help them use soil wisely.

Visual Summary

People depend on natural resources. That is why it is important to conserve them.

Natural Resource	Ways People Use It	
rocks	building	fuel
water	drinking	electricity
soils	building	growing plants
plants	building	food

My Journal

Review your answers to the Lesson Preview questions.

STANDARDS 3.c., 3.e.

Main Ideas

1. Explain how rocks provide fuel. **(p. 132)**

2. What are five ways people use water? **(pp. 142–143)**

3. What makes soil fertile? **(p. 148)**

Vocabulary

Choose the correct word from the box.

4. To use less of something to make it last longer

5. A way to bring water to dry land

6. Something found in nature that people need or use

7. To collect items made of materials that can be used to make new items

natural resource (p. 132)

irrigation (p. 144)

conserve (p. 156)

recycle (p. 158)

Using Science Skills

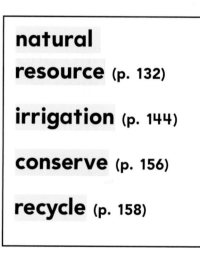

8. Use a hand lens to look at something made from rock or soil. Draw what you see.

9. **Critical Thinking** Your houseplant needs dry conditions. In what kind of soil should you plant it? Tell why.

STANDARDS 1–2: 3.e.; 3: 3.c.; 4–7: 3.e.; 8: 3.a., 4.f.; 9: 3.c.

165

Test Practice

Choose the correct answer.

1. Which of these is a natural resource?

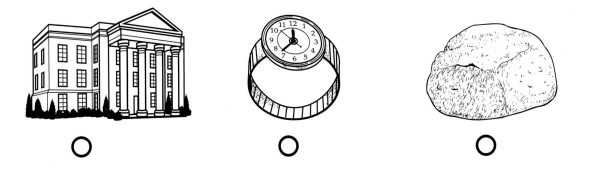

   ○   ○   ○

2. Wind and water breaking large rocks into smaller pieces is called _____.

   erosion   weathering   gravity

   ○   ○   ○

3. What probably made this fossil?

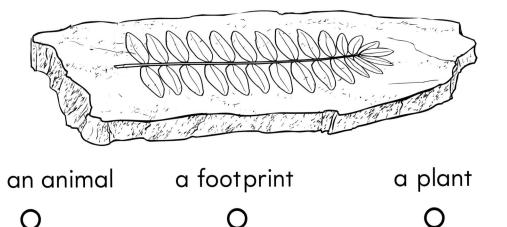

   an animal   a footprint   a plant

   ○   ○   ○

4. Fertile soils are rich in _____.

air   humus   sand

○   ○   ○

5. What are rocks made of?

plants   humus   minerals

○   ○   ○

Write the correct answer.

6. How are rocks alike and different?

7. Name three natural resources and a way you use each one.

STANDARDS 1: 3.e., 2: 3.b., 3: 3.d.,
4: 3.c., 5–6: 3.a., 7: 3.e.

167

You Can...

Discover More

When can you see through rocks?

You can see through rocks if the rocks are made into glass. First, sand, limestone, and soda ash are mixed together. They are put in a hot furnace until they melt. Then, as the mixture cools, glass objects can be formed.

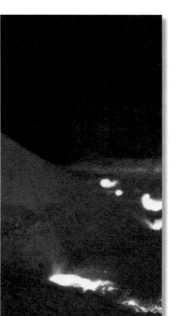

Simulations Go to **www.eduplace.com/cascp** to solve more rock riddles.

PHYSICAL UNIT C SCIENCE

Motion and Forces

California Connection

Visit www.eduplace.com/cascp to find out more about motion and forces in California.

Let's Go!

California Field Trip

Spirit of Sacramento

The Spirit of Sacramento only travels about 6 miles (9 km) an hour.

The force of the paddle wheel pushing on the water moves the boat forward.

Paddles help this boy move his kayak through the water.

Motion and Forces

Reading in Science 170

Chapter 5
Objects in Motion 172

Independent Books
- **Objects in Motion**
- **Hide and Seek**
- **Going to the Races**

Chapter 6
Forces 198

Independent Books
- **Forces**
- **Moving Day**
- **Push or Pull**

Motion on a playground

Standard Set 1.
Physical Sciences

The motion of objects can be observed and measured.

THE STEAM SHOVEL

by Rowena Bennett

The steam digger
Is much bigger
Than the biggest beast I know.
He snorts and roars
Like the dinosaurs
That lived long years ago.

He crouches low
On his tractor paws
And scoops the dirt up
With his jaws;
Then swings his long
Stiff neck around
And spits it out
Upon the ground.

Chapter 5

Objects in Motion

San Francisco cable car

LESSON 1

The ball is next to the car. What other position words can you use to describe the location of the ball?

LESSON 2

These boys will run a race. As they race, how will you know who is faster?

My Journal

Write or draw in your journal to answer the questions above.

Vocabulary

position p. 178

distance p. 180

motion p. 186

speed p. 190

Picture Glossary
English-Spanish p. H18

Vocabulary Skill

Use Words

position

The ball's position is under the table.

Use clues from the sentence above to help you understand what the word **position** means.

position
Position is a place or location.

distance
Distance is the length of space between two people, places, or things.

speed
Speed is the distance an object moves in a set amount of time.

motion

An object that is in motion changes its position, or moves from one place to another.

Start with Your Standards

Standard Set 1. Physical Sciences

1.a. *Students know* the position of an object can be described by locating it in relation to another object or to the background.

1.b. *Students know* an object's motion can be described by recording the change in position of the object over time.

Standard Set 4. Investigation and Experimentation covered in this chapter: 4.b., 4.e.

How Can You Describe an Object's Position?

Building Background

Distance and position can be used to show one object's location in relation to another object.

Inquiry Skill

Measure Use tools and metric units to find length.

STANDARDS

1.a. *Students know* the position of an object can be described by locating it in relation to another object or to the background.
4.b. Measure length, weight, temperature, and liquid volume with appropriate tools and express those measurements in standard metric system units.

What You Need

book

classroom objects

meter stick

Location of Objects		
Object	Distance from Book	Location in Relation to Book

recording chart

Locate an Object

Steps

1. Place a book on a table or on the floor. Be careful not to move the book.

2. Place three objects around the book.

3. **Measure** Use a meter stick. Measure how far each object is from the book. Record the distance in a chart.

4. **Record Data** Write the location of each object in relation to the book.

STEP 1

STEP 2

STEP 3

Think and Share

1. **Compare** How did the location of the objects vary?

2. **Classify** Which object was farthest from the book?

Guided Inquiry

Experiment Move the book to a new location. Leave the other objects where they are. **Measure** how far each object is from the book. Record your measurements.

Vocabulary

position

distance

Reading Skill

Draw Conclusions

Fact Fact

Conclusion

STANDARDS

1.a. *Students know* the position of an object can be described by locating it in relation to another object or to the background.

Describing Position

One way to describe an object is by its position. **Position** is a place or location. To describe an object's position, you can compare the object's location to that of another object. You can describe the objects in this room by comparing their locations.

Draw Conclusions Why can more than one position word be used to describe an object?

to the left of the bank

on the desk

under the bank and over the books

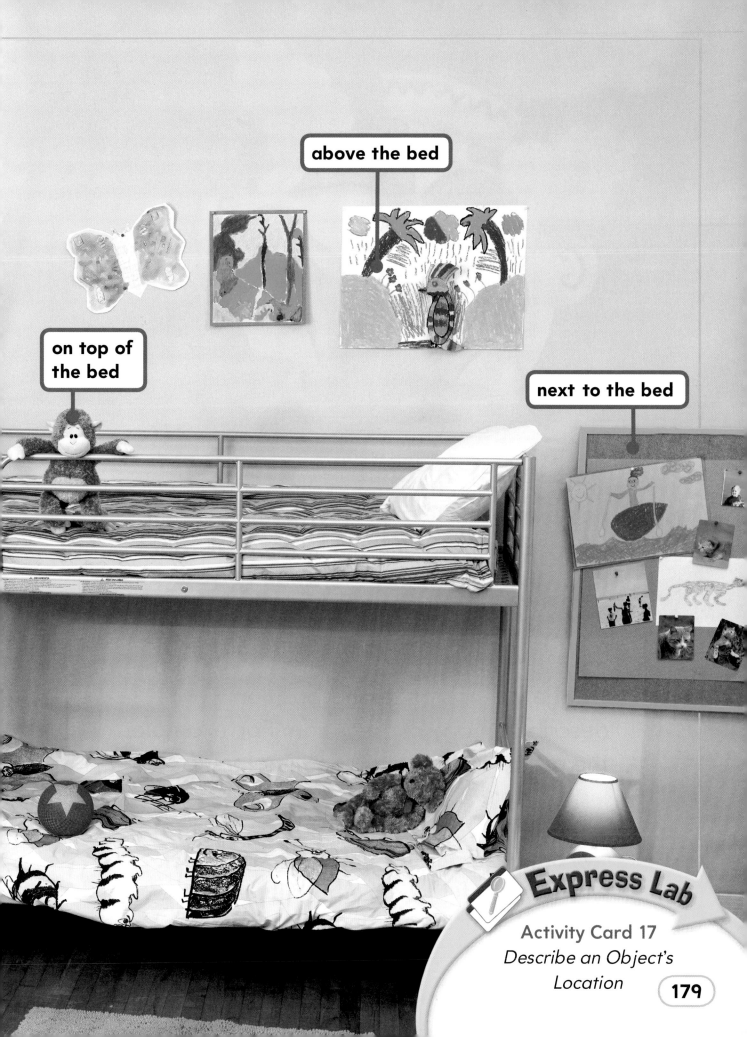

above the bed

on top of the bed

next to the bed

Express Lab

Activity Card 17
Describe an Object's Location

Measuring Distance

You can locate an object by measuring its distance from another object. **Distance** is the length of space between two people, places, or things. You can use a ruler or meter stick to measure distance.

Together, distance and position words describe an object's location. For example, the red ball is about 10 centimeters to the left of Hole 2.

Draw Conclusions To locate an object, why is it helpful to know both its position and its distance from another object?

How can you describe the location of the yellow ball?

The green ball is 5 centimeters to the right of Hole 2.

Lesson Wrap-Up

❶ **Vocabulary** What is **distance**?

❷ 🎯**Reading Skill** How can position words help you know an object's location?

❸ **Measure** How can a meter stick help you tell the location of an object?

🔲 **Technology** Visit **www.eduplace.com/cascp** to find out more about positions of objects.

STANDARDS 1–2: 1.a., 3: 1.a., 4.b.

Measuring Tools Then and Now

People have been measuring for thousands of years. At first, people used common objects or parts of their bodies as measuring tools. They began to see a need for standard units of measurement.

About 200 years ago, France began using the metric system. Today, most countries use the metric system.

More than 1,000 years ago, a yard was the length of a man's belt. But belts were different lengths.

About 900 years ago, King Henry I of England ruled that a yard was the distance from his nose to his thumb.

STANDARDS

1.a. *Students know* the position of an object can be described by locating it in relation to another object or to the background.

MATH **LINK**

The children are using a meter stick to measure distance.

Today, all meter sticks are modeled after this metal bar that France sent to the United States.

Sharing Ideas

1. **Write About It** How did people solve the problem of having different units of measurement?

2. **Talk About It** Why is it important that different countries use the same kind of measurement?

How Can You Describe an Object's Motion?

Building Background

An object's motion and position can change over time. An object that travels farther than another in a set amount of time is moving faster.

Inquiry Skill

Work Together You can work as a team to share ideas and still think for yourself about what you observe.

STANDARDS

1.b. *Students know* an object's motion can be described by recording the change in position of the object over time.
4.e. Construct bar graphs to record data, using appropriately labeled axes.

What You Need

wind-up toys

tape and stopwatch

string and ruler

bar graph

Objects in Motion

Steps

STEP 1

1. **Work Together** Place a piece of tape on the floor. Wind up a toy. Place it on the tape. Start the stopwatch.

2. **Measure** Every five seconds, mark the toy's position with tape. Stop after 20 seconds.

STEP 2

3. **Record Data** Use string to trace the toy's path. Measure the length of the string. Record the results on a bar graph.

4. Repeat Steps 1–3 with two other toys.

STEP 3

Think and Share

1. **Work Together** Talk with a partner. What did you observe about motion and position?

2. **Draw Conclusions** What can you conclude about the toy that went the farthest?

Guided Inquiry

Experiment Repeat the activity. Did you get the same results? **Communicate** your observations to others.

▶ **Vocabulary**

motion

speed

◎ **Reading Skill**
Compare and Contrast

Compare	Contrast

▲ **STANDARDS**

1.b. *Students know* an object's motion can be described by recording the change in position of the object over time.
1.a. *Students know* the position of an object can be described by locating it in relation to another object or to the background.

Motion of an Object

The motion of objects can be observed. An object that is in **motion** changes its position, or moves from one place to another. An object can move in a straight line, back and forth, up and down, or even in a circle.

To tell if an object is moving, compare its position to objects in the background that are not moving. If the background changes, you know that the object is moving.

moving in a circle

How is the background different in these photos?

The buildings and trees along a street do not move. Look at the photos. You can tell that the cable car has moved because its position on the street has changed. The background in the second photo is different from the background in the first photo.

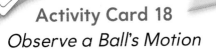

Compare and Contrast Describe the position of the cable car in the two photos.

Express Lab

Activity Card 18
Observe a Ball's Motion

Measuring Motion

The motion of objects can be measured in different ways. You can measure the distance that a person or an object travels. For example, a swimmer may travel a distance of 50 meters, 100 meters, and so on.

You can also measure the time it takes to go a set distance. In a swimming race, a stopwatch is used to find the time it takes each swimmer to go a set distance.

It takes more time to go a longer distance.

Fastest Swimming Times	
Distance	**Time**
50 meters	about 22 seconds
100 meters	about 48 seconds
200 meters	about 1 minute 44 seconds
400 meters	about 3 minutes 40 seconds

In a swimming race, the swimmers start at the same time. They swim the same distance.

Look at the photo. The swimmer on the right finished first. He swam the set distance in less time than the other swimmer. To finish first, the swimmer moved faster.

◎ Compare and Contrast

What is the difference between a fast swimmer and a slow swimmer?

Speed

You can describe motion in terms of speed. **Speed** is the distance an object moves in a set amount of time. Speed tells you how fast or slow something is moving. Different objects move at different speeds.

Compare Speeds

Different things move at different speeds.

snail

bike

rabbit

car

The cheetah is the fastest land animal. Some cheetahs can run almost as fast as a car can move.

Compare and Contrast How would you compare the speeds of a snail and a rabbit?

Lesson Wrap-Up

❶ **Vocabulary** What tells you how fast or slow an object is moving?

❷ **Reading Skill** How can comparing an object to its background help you tell that the object moved?

❸ **Work Together** How is it helpful to work as a team when measuring moving objects?

Technology Visit **www.eduplace.com/cascp** to find out more about motion.

STANDARDS 1: 1.b., 2: 1.a., 3: 1.b.

STANDARDS **1.b.** *Students know* an object's motion can be described by recording the change in position of the object over time.

Fast, Faster, Fastest!

How would you like to ride in a car that is faster than many jet airplanes? Meet the Thrust SSC, the fastest car in the world!

The Thrust SSC uses two jet engines for power. It set a world record by reaching a top speed of 1,227 kilometers per hour.

The Thrust SSC can travel the distance of three football fields in less than a second!

The world record was set on a dry salt lake at Black Rock Desert, Nevada.

My Journal

In your journal, use numbers or drawings to show how many football fields the Thrust travels in five seconds.

LINKS for Home and School

Math Measure Distances

Use a meter stick to measure the distance from the door to different objects in the classroom. Record data in a chart.

Classroom Distances	
Object	Distance to Door

1. Which object is closest to the door?

2. Which object is farthest away from the door?

Writing Describe a Race

Write or draw a story about a race. Describe the setting, the people, and the event. Tell who wins and why.

Animator

An animator makes cartoon characters seem to come to life. Animators must understand position and motion.

An animator draws pictures or makes models. Each one is just a little different from the last. Filming the pictures or models one after another makes them seem to move.

What It Takes!

- Talent in art and design
- Good math skills

Visual Summary

An object can be described by its position and its motion.

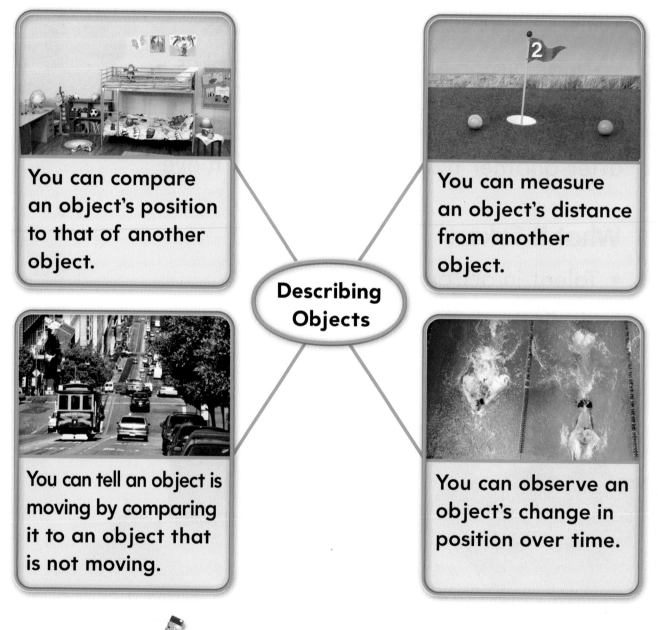

You can compare an object's position to that of another object.

You can measure an object's distance from another object.

Describing Objects

You can tell an object is moving by comparing it to an object that is not moving.

You can observe an object's change in position over time.

 My Journal

Review your answers to the Lesson Preview questions.

 STANDARDS 1.a., 1.b.

Main Ideas

1. How can distance help locate an object? (p. 180)

2. How can you tell that an object is moving? (p. 186)

3. What are two ways to measure motion? (p. 188)

Vocabulary

Choose the correct word from the box.

4. The distance an object moves in a set amount of time

5. A place or location

6. An object's change in position or location

7. The length of space between two people, places, or things

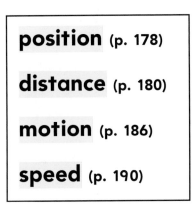

position (p. 178)
distance (p. 180)
motion (p. 186)
speed (p. 190)

Using Science Skills

8. You make a graph of the distances that three objects moved. What labels do you use?

9. **Critical Thinking** You know how far away an object is from another object. But you still can't find it. Explain why.

STANDARDS 1: 1.a., 2–4: 1.b., 5: 1.a., 6: 1.b., 7: 1.a., 8: 4.e., 9: 1.a.

197

Chapter 6

Forces

Playing soccer

LESSON 1

People use a cart to carry things. How do they make it move?

LESSON 2

A volleyball player can change a ball's direction. How can she do that?

LESSON 3

This mallet can push the ball. What other tools can make work easier?

LESSON 4

Leaves fall from a tree. What makes leaves fall down to the ground?

My Journal

Write or draw in your journal to answer the questions above.

Vocabulary

force p. 204

energy p. 206

friction p. 208

direction p. 212

pulley p. 223

gravity p. 230

weight p. 232

Picture Glossary
English-Spanish p. H18

Vocabulary Skill

Find All the Meanings

direction

A word can have more than one meaning. You may know that a **direction** is an instruction. The word **direction** also is the path an object follows.

force
A force is a push or a pull.

friction
Friction is a force that makes an object slow down.

pulley
A pulley is a wheel with a groove through which a rope or chain moves.

gravity

Gravity is a force that pulls all objects toward each other.

Start with Your Standards

Standard Set 1. Physical Sciences

1.c. *Students know* the way to change how something is moving is by giving it a push or a pull. The size of the change is related to the strength, or the amount of force, of the push or pull.

1.d. *Students know* tools and machines are used to apply pushes and pulls (forces) to make things move.

1.e. *Students know* objects fall to the ground unless something holds them up.

Standard Set 4. Investigation and Experimentation covered in this chapter: 4.a., 4.b., 4.d., 4.g.

What Do Forces Do?

Building Background

A push or a pull is needed to move an object. The amount of force affects the movement of the object.

Inquiry Skill

Measure Use tools and metric units to find length.

STANDARDS

1.c. *Students know* the way to change how something is moving is by giving it a push or a pull. The size of the change is related to the strength, or the amount of force, of the push or pull.
4.b. Measure length, weight, temperature, and liquid volume with appropriate tools and express those measurements in standard metric system units.

What You Need

goggles

chair

tape and meter stick

cart and rubber band

Change Motion

Steps

STEP 1

1. **Measure** Place a line of tape on the floor. Place two more lines 15 and 30 centimeters behind the first. Put a chair leg even with the first line. Put a rubber band around the chair leg and stretch it. **Safety:** Wear goggles!

STEP 2

2. **Observe** Place a cart against the band. Pull it back to the second line and let go. Use tape to mark where it stops. Measure and record the distance the cart traveled.

STEP 3

3. **Measure** Repeat Step 2, but this time pull the cart back to the third line.

Think and Share

1. **Compare** When did the cart travel farther?

2. **Infer** What caused the cart to travel farther?

Guided Inquiry

Experiment Tape an object to the cart. Repeat the activity. **Compare** the results.

Vocabulary

force
energy
friction

Reading Skill
Cause and Effect

Cause ➔ Effect

STANDARDS

1.c. *Students know* the way to change how something is moving is by giving it a push or a pull. The size of the change is related to the strength, or the amount of force, of the push or pull.

Pushes and Pulls

Any time an object moves from one position to another there is motion. An object that is not moving is at rest. It will stay at rest unless a force makes it move. A **force** is a push or a pull. A force changes the position of an object.

The cat in the picture below uses force to move the ball of yarn. At first, the ball of yarn is not moving. Then, the cat puts the yarn in motion.

How did the cat make the ball of yarn move?

yarn at rest   yarn in motion

A force changes the motion of an object. A push moves an object away from you. A pull moves an object toward you. The chair in the picture is being pulled. The bookcase is being pushed.

Cause and Effect What kind of force causes an object to move toward you?

These children are using forces to move the furniture in the room.

PULL

PUSH

Size of a Force

Different size forces are needed to move objects of different sizes. A large force is needed to move a heavy object. A smaller force can move a lighter object.

When you push or pull an object, you give the object energy. **Energy** is the ability to cause change. The amount of energy depends on the size of the force.

large push

small push

Which kick will make the ball move farther?

A large force gives an object more energy. If you kick a ball with a lot of force, the ball moves fast and goes far. If you kick the same ball with less force, the ball moves more slowly for a shorter distance.

Cause and Effect If you hit a ball with only a little force, what will happen?

Express Lab

Activity Card 19
Measure Motion

Friction between the brakes and the wheel stops the bike.

Friction

Friction is a force that makes an object slow down when it rubs against another object. Friction is a kind of pull. There is more friction when an object moves across a rough surface than across a smooth surface.

 Cause and Effect What kind of surface causes more friction?

smooth   rough   rougher

less friction   more friction

This slide has a smooth surface. There is little friction when the soft cloth moves across the smooth slide. Less friction makes the ride faster.

Lesson Wrap-Up

❶ Vocabulary What is a **force**?

❷ 🎯 Reading Skill What happens when a bicycle moves from a smooth surface to a rough surface?

❸ Measure How does measuring help you find out what kind of force moves an object farther?

🖥 **Technology** Visit **www.eduplace.com/cascp** to find out more about forces.

STANDARDS 1–3: 1.c.

How Can You Change an Object's Direction?

Building Background

A push or pull is needed to change the direction of an object's motion. A force is also needed to change an object's speed.

Inquiry Skill

Predict Instead of guessing, use patterns you observe to tell what you think will happen.

ball

tape

string

STANDARDS

1.c. *Students know* the way to change how something is moving is by giving it a push or a pull. The size of the change is related to the strength, or the amount of force, of the push or pull.
4.a. Make predictions based on observed patterns and not random guessing.

Change Direction

Steps

1. Sit on the floor across from a classmate. Put a tape mark on the floor for a starting line.

2. **Observe** Roll the ball to the classmate. Have the classmate push the ball when it gets close. Use tape to mark the place where the ball changes direction.

3. Use tape to mark where the ball stops. Then use string to show how the ball moved.

4. Switch roles and repeat Steps 1–3.

STEP 1

STEP 2

STEP 3

Think and Share

1. **Infer** Why did the ball change direction?

2. **Predict** In what direction will a ball move the next time you push it?

Guided Inquiry

Experiment Move a different object. **Predict** how it will change direction when you push it. Draw or write about each step you take to make the object move.

Learn by Reading

Vocabulary

direction

Reading Skill

Sequence

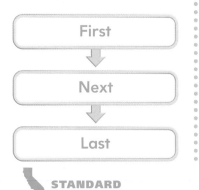

First

↓

Next

↓

Last

STANDARD

1.c. *Students know* the way to change how something is moving is by giving it a push or a pull. The size of the change is related to the strength, or the amount of force, of the push or pull.

The ball rolls to the kicker. Her kick is a push. The push makes the ball change direction.

Express Lab

Activity Card 20
Change an Object's Direction

Change Direction

A force can change the direction of a motion. **Direction** is the path that an object follows. When you bounce a ball, you push it in a direction away from your hand. The ball keeps moving until it hits the ground. Then it changes direction when it bounces up.

Sequence Tell how a ball changes direction when it is bounced.

The kicked ball moves in the direction of this player. Catching the ball is a push. Catching the ball stops its motion.

This player pushes the ball when he rolls it. His push starts a motion in the direction of the kicker.

Change Speed

A force can change the speed of an object. A large force gives an object more energy. When you ride a scooter, you give it a push with one foot. You change the speed of the scooter. A stronger push will make the scooter go faster. The pull of friction as the wheels rub against the pavement will slow down the scooter.

Sequence What happens after you give a push with your foot while riding a scooter?

What can the boy do to change his speed?

Brakes are used to slow a moving object. The skater pushes the brake against the ground. The brake rubbing against the ground makes friction. The friction slowly pulls the skater to a stop.

Lesson Wrap-Up

❶ **Vocabulary** What is **direction**?

❷ 🎯**Reading Skill** How can you speed up and then slow down on a scooter?

❸ **Predict** A child kicks a ball toward a wall. What will happen when the ball hits the wall?

⌨ **Technology** Visit **www.eduplace.com/cascp** to find out more about motion.

STANDARDS 1–2: 1.c., 3: 1.c., 4.a.

Motion at the California Speedway

Racecars move very fast. Let's listen and learn about motion at the California Speedway.

Cast
Reporter
Driver 1
Driver 2
Driver 3
Flagman

Reporter: Hi, race fans! I'm here at the California Speedway talking to a few drivers before today's race. First, I'll ask the drivers to tell me about the track.

Driver 1: The track is two miles long.

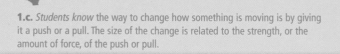

STANDARDS

1.c. *Students know* the way to change how something is moving is by giving it a push or a pull. The size of the change is related to the strength, or the amount of force, of the push or pull.

READING LINK

Reporter: How fast do you think you might go?

Driver 1: I may go more than 180 miles an hour on the straight part of the track.

Reporter: Wow, that's fast! How do you do that?

Driver 2: The tires push against the track and the car starts moving forward.

Driver 3: That's right. A big engine helps.

Reporter: Does a big engine make a car go fast?

Driver 2: Yes. A big engine will make the back wheels push against the track with more force.

Driver 3: And the bigger the push, the faster something moves.

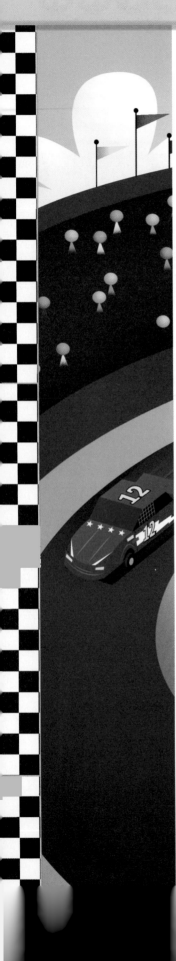

Reporter: How long is the race?

Flagman: It's a 500-mile race. When I wave the green flag, the race starts. The cars go around the track 250 times.

Reporter: You're making me dizzy! How long will that take?

Driver 1: That depends. Sometimes we have to slow down if there is a problem on the track.

Reporter: What kind of problem?

Driver 2: Sometimes a driver does not pull the wheel enough to turn the car. It just keeps going straight. Then it might bump into another car.

Driver 3: If two cars bump into each other, that's a big force. The force could make the cars spin and change direction.

Flagman: That's where I come in. I wave the yellow flag. All the cars slow down until the track is clear. Then I wave the green flag when the cars can speed up again.

Reporter: Who do you think will win?

Driver 3: I hope I will be the fastest. The fastest one will be the winner. The fastest driver is the driver who finishes all 250 laps ahead of everyone else.

Flagman: Watch for the checkered flag. Then you will know that the race is over.

Sharing Ideas

1. **Write About It** How do forces and motions change when you are riding in a car?

2. **Talk About It** How is car racing like bicycle riding with friends?

What Do Tools and Machines Do?

Building Background

Tools and machines can be used to help move objects.

Inquiry Skill

Ask Questions When you ask questions about what you observe, you can learn more about the world.

STANDARDS

1.d. *Students know* tools and machines are used to apply pushes and pulls (forces) to make things move.
4.d. Write or draw descriptions of a sequence of steps, events, and observations.

What You Need

cup with handle

rocks

spool and pencil

string and tape

Tools Push and Pull

Steps

1 Put a cup on the floor. Fill it with rocks. Tie a string to the handle. Make the cup move up.

STEP 1

2 **Work Together** Make a pulley. Slide a spool onto a pencil. Tape one end of the pencil to the edge of a table. Stretch the string from the cup over the spool.

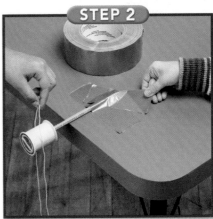
STEP 2

3 Use the pulley to make the cup move up.

4 **Record Data** Draw a series of pictures to show how you moved the cup each time.

STEP 3

Think and Share

1. **Infer** What kind of force did you use to move the cup of rocks?

2. **Compare** How did the pulley change the force?

Guided Inquiry

Ask Questions What are some other tools that can help move objects? Ask someone who knows about tools. **Communicate** what you learn with others.

Vocabulary

pulley

⌖ **Reading Skill**

Main Idea and Details

Main
Idea

Detail   Detail

STANDARD

1.d. *Students know* tools and machines are used to apply pushes and pulls (forces) to make things move.

Tools and Machines

Some kinds of work can be done with just your hands. For other kinds of work, people use tools and machines. Tools and machines make work easier by changing the force in some way.

Some tools make pushing easier. A hammer pushes a nail through wood. The force of the hammer moves the nail. It takes less force to move the nail with the hammer than to move it without a hammer.

A hammer makes the force of a person's arm greater.

Sometimes it is easier to pull down than to push or lift up. A **pulley** is a wheel with a groove through which a rope or chain moves. You pull down on the rope on one side and the object on the other side goes up.

🎯 **Main Idea** In what ways does a machine change force?

A pulley changes the direction of a force, but not its strength.

The man pulls down on the rope. In which direction does the bird feeder move?

Applying Forces

Most tools and machines allow people to work more quickly or more easily. Some tools and machines allow people to apply forces they would not be able to apply by themselves. If an object is too heavy to move, a machine can be used. Some machines have motors to help apply a force.

Main Idea Why do people need machines for some work?

▲ A wrench pushes a bolt and causes it to turn. This tool helps control how the bolt is being moved.

A car engine uses a force to turn the wheels. The wheels cause the car to move. ▼

A bat is a tool used to push a ball. When a bat hits a pitched ball, it changes the direction of the ball's motion.

Lesson Wrap-Up

❶ Vocabulary How does a **pulley** work?

❷ 🎯 Reading Skill What are tools and machines used for?

❸ Ask Questions How can asking questions help you find out what tools and machines do?

💻 Technology Visit **www.eduplace.com/cascp** to find out more about tools and machines.

STANDARDS 1–3: 1.d.

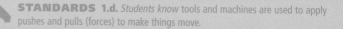

MEGA MOVER

Meet the mightiest earthmover ever made! It is 95 meters high and 215 meters long. That's taller than the Statue of Liberty and longer than two football fields! The bucket wheel is taller than a four-story building. Each bucket scoops 15 tons of earth. That is the weight of three elephants!

The mega earthmover could fill more than 2,000 very large dump trucks in a day.

My Journal

In your journal, use numbers or drawings to show how many elephants ten mega-buckets could carry.

227

What Makes Things Fall?

Building Background

The force of gravity pulls objects. An object will fall to the ground unless something holds it up.

Inquiry Skill

Experiment When you experiment, you choose the items you will need and plan the steps you will follow.

STANDARDS

1.e. *Students know* objects fall to the ground unless something holds them up.
4.g. Follow oral instructions for a scientific investigation.

What You Need

egg in a plastic bag

newspaper

tape

Falling Objects

Steps

① **Work Together** Design a landing pad that will keep a falling egg from breaking. Use only tape and newspaper.

STEP 1

② **Work Together** Build the landing pad that your group designed. Share your group's design with the class.

STEP 2

③ **Experiment** Hold the egg above the landing pad. It should be near your waist. Drop the egg. Observe the results. Share your results with the class.

STEP 3

Think and Share

1. **Infer** What caused the egg to drop?

2. What can you infer about the landing pads that kept the eggs from breaking?

Guided Inquiry

Experiment Make a plan to drop the egg from different heights. **Record** the steps of your plan. Read the steps aloud. Have classmates follow them.

▶ **Vocabulary**

gravity

weight

◎ **Reading Skill**

Draw Conclusions

Fact
↓
Fact
↓
Conclusion

🏴 **STANDARD**

1.e. *Students know* objects fall to the ground unless something holds them up.

Gravity causes water to move downhill.

Gravity

If you drop a ball, gravity causes it to fall to the ground. **Gravity** is a force that pulls all objects toward each other. Earth pulls on the ball, and the ball pulls on Earth. The ball is much easier to move than Earth, so the ball falls. Gravity causes objects near Earth's surface to fall to the ground.

Vernal Falls in Yosemite National Park

Gravity pulls on the glass and the juice inside it. The table holds the glass up and stops it from falling. When the glass is pushed off the table, the glass and juice fall toward Earth.

⊙ Draw Conclusions You throw a ball up into the air. Then it falls down. Why does this happen?

Gravity and Weight

Weight is a measure of the pull of gravity on an object. The pull of gravity is stronger on objects that have more mass.

Mass is a measure of the amount of material in an object. A large rock has a lot of mass. The pull of gravity on the rock is strong. It weighs a lot. A feather has little mass. The pull of gravity is not as strong. A feather weighs less than a rock.

Which pail has the greater weight? How can you tell?

The rock is heavier than the feather.

The toy elephant has more mass than the toy cheetah does. The toy elephant weighs more because gravity pulls harder on it.

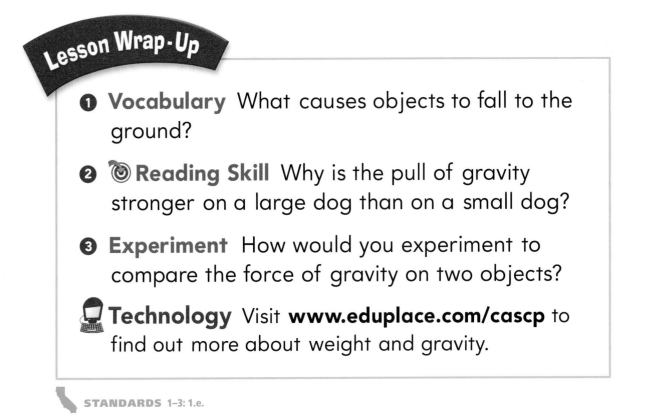

Draw Conclusions How can you tell that one object is heavier than another?

Lesson Wrap-Up

❶ **Vocabulary** What causes objects to fall to the ground?

❷ **Reading Skill** Why is the pull of gravity stronger on a large dog than on a small dog?

❸ **Experiment** How would you experiment to compare the force of gravity on two objects?

Technology Visit **www.eduplace.com/cascp** to find out more about weight and gravity.

Math Make a Table

Use a balance to find the mass of five different objects. Record the data in a table.

Object	Mass

1. Which object had the most mass?

2. Which object would be pulled more by gravity?

Writing Describe an Object

Write about an object that moves. Describe how it moves. Make a drawing of the object in motion.

Dr. Ellen Ochoa

Dr. Ellen Ochoa works for NASA. She is proud to have been the first Hispanic woman astronaut. She has visited space four times.

Dr. Ochoa remembers growing up in La Mesa, California. Today, she likes to talk to children at schools. Her message is to work hard to reach your goals.

There is no gravity in space. Foot straps keep Dr. Ochoa from floating.

Visual Summary

Forces make objects start moving and change direction. Forces also make objects speed up and slow down. Tools and machines can change a force.

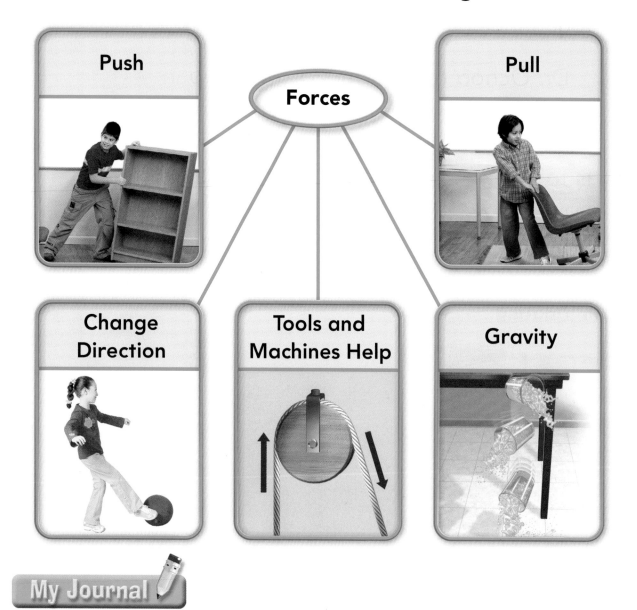

Push

Forces

Pull

Change Direction

Tools and Machines Help

Gravity

My Journal

Review your answers to the Lesson Preview questions.

STANDARDS 1.c., 1.d., 1.e.

Main Ideas

1. How do you change the position of an object? (p. 204)

2. How does a big push change an object's motion? (p. 214)

3. How is a tool or machine helpful? (p. 222)

Vocabulary

Choose the correct word from the box.

4. A force that makes an object slow down when it rubs against another object

5. A wheel with a groove through which a rope or chain moves

6. The path that an object follows

7. The ability to cause change

energy (p. 206)
friction (p. 208)
direction (p. 212)
pulley (p. 223)

Using Science Skills

8. What tool would you use to measure the distance that an object travels?

9. **Critical Thinking** How does Earth's gravity affect objects that are not supported?

STANDARDS 1–2: 1.c., 3: 1.d., 4: 1.c., 5: 1.d., 6–7: 1.c., 8: 4.b., 9: 1.e.

237

Choose the correct answer.

1. Which picture shows that the crayon is to the right of the paper?

     ○   ○   ○

2. You know an object is in motion because it changes its _____.

motion   position   shape

  ○   ○   ○

3. You can change the way something moves by giving it a _____.

push   speed   mass

  ○   ○   ○

4. An object that makes pushing and pulling easier is a _____.

machine   ball   force

  ○   ○   ○

5. Giving a push or pull can change the _____ of a moving ball.

shape   gravity   direction
O   O   O

6. Earth's gravity causes objects to fall _____.

up   sideways   down
O   O   O

Checking Main Ideas

Write the correct answer.

7. Your pencil rolls off your desk. Tell what will happen and why.

8. Which car is faster? How do you know?

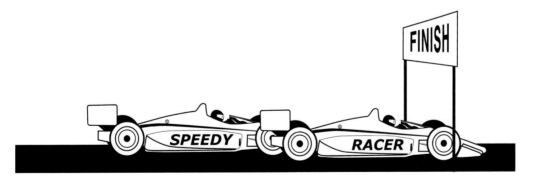

STANDARDS 1: 1.a., 2: 1.b., 3: 1.c., 4: 1.d., 5: 1.c., 6–7: 1.e., 8: 1.b.

You Can...

Discover More

What is the fastest speed that a human can run?

At the 1996 Olympics, a man ran 200 meters in 19.32 seconds. That's about 37 kilometers an hour. But compared with a cheetah, humans are slow. A cheetah can run three times as fast as a human, or almost 112 kilometers per hour!

Simulations Go to **www.eduplace.com/cascp** to see animals and objects that move quickly and slowly.

PHYSICAL SCIENCE

UNIT D

Magnets
and
Sound

California Connection

Visit www.eduplace.com/cascp
to find out more about magnets
and sound in California.

Mariachi Festival

Mariachi music combines music from Spain, Mexico, and Africa. This festival is at the Hollywood Bowl.

Mariachi violins often play the melody, or tune, of a song.

Each of the six strings on a guitarron plays a different sound.

Magnets and Sound

Reading in Science 242

Chapter 7
Magnets 244

Independent Books
- Magnets
- Magnet Time
- Magnet Games

Chapter 8
Making Sound 272

Independent Books
- Making Sound
- What's a Kazoo?
- How Does This Sound?

Iron filings on a horseshoe magnet

The motion of objects can be observed and measured.

Magnets

Magnets push and pull;
They attract and repel.
They attract objects made with iron,
And they do it oh so well.

But my coat and water bottle
Are things magnets don't attract.
There's no push, there's no pull,
And that's a fact.

 from *Science Songs*, track 25

Chapter 7

Magnets

Groceries
eggs
milk
bread

Baseball
Game at
6:00 PM

Refrigerator magnets

LESSON 1

A magnet pulls paper clips and some other objects toward it. Why does this happen?

LESSON 2

The filings make a pattern around a magnet. Where is a magnet's force strongest?

LESSON 3

Magnets can make things move without touching them. How do you think this happens?

My Journal

Write or draw in your journal to answer the questions above.

Vocabulary

magnet p. 250

attract p. 250

magnetic p. 250

poles p. 252

repels p. 253

magnetic field p. 258

magnetic force p. 262

Picture Glossary

English-Spanish p. H18

Vocabulary Skill

Use Opposites

attract

repel

These words are opposites. **Attract** means to pull toward. What do you think **repel** means?

attract
When objects attract, they pull toward each other.

poles
The poles are the places on a magnet where the forces are strongest.

magnetic field
The space around a magnet where the magnet's force works is a magnetic field.

magnetic
If an object and a magnet attract each other, the object is magnetic.

Start with Your Standards

Standard Set 1. Physical Sciences

1.f. *Students know* magnets can be used to make some objects move without being touched.

Standard Set 4. Investigation and Experimentation covered in this chapter: 4.a., 4.d.

What Are Magnets?

Building Background

Magnets can pull toward each other or push away from each other. Magnets attract objects made of iron and steel.

Inquiry Skill

Observe Use your senses and tools to find out about something.

STANDARDS

1.f. *Students know* magnets can be used to make some objects move without being touched.
4.d. Write or draw descriptions of a sequence of steps, events, and observations.

What You Need

2 bar magnets

Test Magnets

Steps

1 **Observe** Hold an end of one magnet near an end of the other magnet. Observe what happens.

2 **Record data** Write or draw your observations on a chart like the one shown.

3 **Experiment** Turn one magnet around. Hold it near the other magnet. Observe. Write or draw what happened next.

4 Turn the other magnet around. Observe. Write or draw what happened next.

Think and Share

1. **Compare** When was the push or pull stronger?

2. **Infer** How do magnets act on each other?

STEP 1

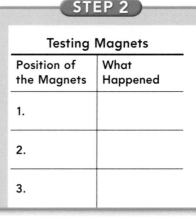
STEP 2

Testing Magnets	
Position of the Magnets	What Happened
1.	
2.	
3.	

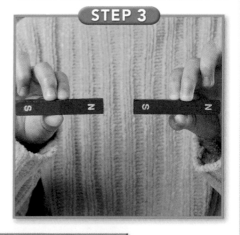
STEP 3

Guided Inquiry

Experiment What if you repeat the activity with horseshoe magnets? **Predict** what will happen. Then try it and share your results with others.

249

▶ **Vocabulary**

magnet

attract

magnetic

poles

repels

◎ **Reading Skill**

Cause and Effect

Cause ➡ Effect

🏴 **STANDARDS**

1.f. *Students know* magnets can be used to make some objects move without being touched.

Which materials does the magnet attract?

Magnets

A **magnet** is an object that attracts iron or steel objects. When objects **attract**, they pull toward each other. Magnets come in many shapes and sizes. They also have many uses. If an object and a magnet attract each other, the object is **magnetic**. Most magnetic objects have a metal in them called iron.

Some objects are not attracted by magnets. If an object is not attracted by a magnet, the object is nonmagnetic. Objects made from glass, wood, plastic, or paper are nonmagnetic. Metal objects that do not have iron or steel in them are nonmagnetic.

magnetic objects

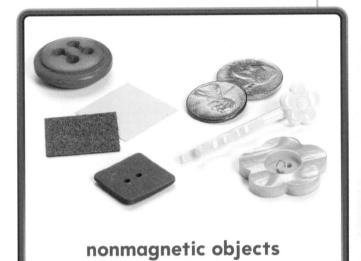

nonmagnetic objects

Cause and Effect Why are some objects attracted by a magnet?

Express Lab

Activity Card 23
Observe Magnets

Magnets Act on Each Other

All magnets have forces that act on other magnets. The force between two magnets can be either a push or a pull. The **poles** are the places on a magnet where the forces are strongest. All magnets have two poles. A magnet does not have to touch an object to push or pull it.

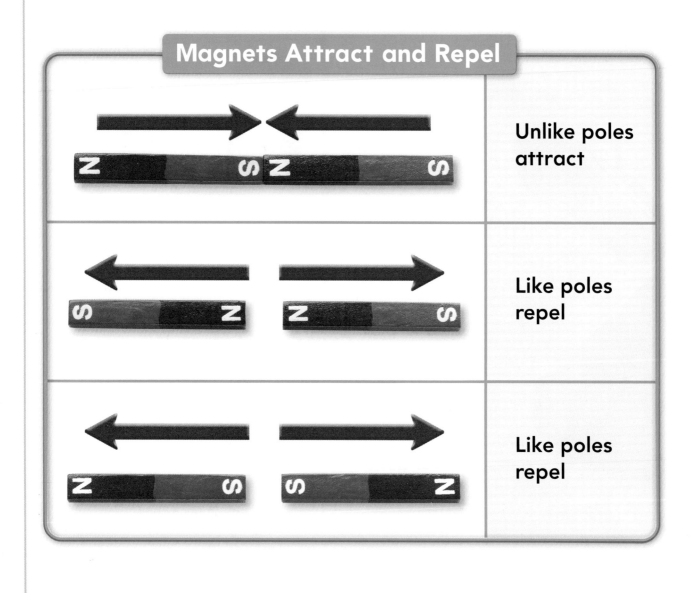

Magnets Attract and Repel

Unlike poles attract

Like poles repel

Like poles repel

On some magnets, the poles are labeled N for north pole and S for south pole. If two unlike poles are near each other, the magnets attract. If two like poles are near each other, the magnets repel. When a magnet **repels**, it pushes an object away from itself.

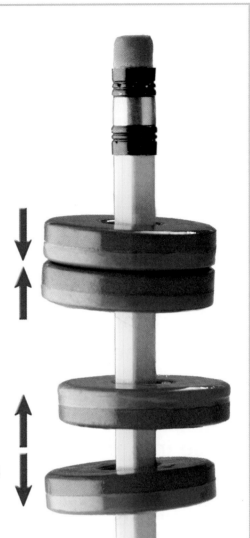

 **Cause and Effect** What happens when like poles are together?

What causes the magnets to be in this position?

Lesson Wrap-Up

❶ **Vocabulary** What is important about the **poles** of a magnet?

❷ **Reading Skill** How should you hold two magnets so they pull toward each other?

❸ **Observe** How can you find the poles of a magnet if they are not labeled?

Technology Visit **www.eduplace.com/cascp** to find out more about magnets.

STANDARDS 1–3: 1.f.

Maglev Trains

Scientists have used what they know about magnets to build a new kind of train. The push and pull of magnets move the maglev. Maglev is short for magnetic levitation. To levitate is to rise into the air and float. The pulling force causes the train to float up to ten centimeters above the track!

People may one day be able to ride maglev trains between the places shown on the map.

To Bakersfield
Palmdale
To Las Vegas, NV
Union Station
Victorville
San Bernardino
LAX
Irvine
Palm Springs
Escondido
San Diego
El Centro

STANDARDS

1.f. *Students know* magnets can be used to make some objects move without being touched.

READING **LINK**

Magnets cause the train to move forward without touching the track. Magnets in the front of the train pull it. Magnets behind the train push it. Together, these forces cause the maglev to move twice as fast as the fastest regular trains.

Magnetic coils along the track attract magnets on the maglev. The coils and magnets never touch.

Magnetic coils in the track

Magnets on the maglev train

Sharing Ideas

1. **Write About It** The magnetic coils in the track attract the magnets on the bottom of a maglev. What does this tell you about the poles of the magnets?

2. **Talk About It** How did scientists help people by inventing the maglev?

What Is a Magnetic Field?

Building Background

Iron filings can be used to see a magnet's magnetic field. Filing patterns show where the force of the magnet is strongest.

Inquiry Skill

Infer Instead of guessing, use what you observe and know to tell what you think.

What You Need

goggles

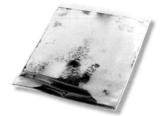

iron filings

bar magnet

Filing Patterns

Steps

STEP 1

1. **Safety:** Wear goggles! Place filings on top of a bar magnet.

2. **Observe** Look at the pattern that the filings make. Write or draw what you see.

STEP 2

3. **Record Data** Move the filings around on top of the magnet. Record what you see.

4. **Predict** Tell what you think you will see if you move the filings again. Test your prediction.

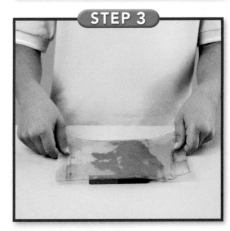

STEP 3

Think and Share

1. **Infer** Why does the pattern change when you move the filings?

2. **Compare** Which part of the magnet attracted most of the filings? Tell why.

Guided Inquiry

Ask Questions Finish this question. How would the pattern look if I used a _____ magnet? **Work together with a partner to find out.**

► **Vocabulary**

magnetic field

 **Reading Skill**

Compare and Contrast

Compare	Contrast

STANDARDS

1.f. *Students know* magnets can be used to make some objects move without being touched.

Magnetic Fields

The space around a magnet where the magnet's force works is a **magnetic field**. A magnet can attract or repel only the objects in its magnetic field.

You cannot see a magnetic field. But you can find it by placing iron filings around a magnet. You can see the pattern that the filings make.

N   S

The iron filings show that the magnetic field is strongest at the poles.

Express Lab

Activity Card 24
Observe a Magnetic Field

A magnet's force is strongest at its poles. The force is strong enough to push or pull objects, even without touching them.

Compare and Contrast How is the center of a magnet different from the poles?

Magnetic objects are pulled to the poles at the ends of this magnet.

Lesson Wrap-Up

1 Vocabulary What is a **magnetic field**?

2 Reading Skill Why do objects hang from the ends of a bar magnet and not from the middle?

3 Infer What can you infer about a magnet by looking at a pattern of iron filings around it?

Technology Visit **www.eduplace.com/cascp** to find out more about magnetic fields.

How Strong Is a Magnet's Force?

Building Background

A magnet's force can attract objects without touching them. Greater distances between a magnet and a magnetic object weaken the force.

Inquiry Skill

Predict Instead of guessing, use patterns you observe to tell what you think will happen.

What You Need

magnet

paper clip on a string

tape

construction paper

STANDARDS

1.f. *Students know* magnets can be used to make some objects move without being touched.
4.a. Make predictions based on observed patterns and not random guessing.

Observe Force

Steps

1. Hang a paper clip from a table edge with string and tape.

STEP 1

2. **Experiment** Wave a magnet under the clip. Observe. Lower the magnet. Wave it again. Keep lowering the magnet. Observe what happens to the clip.

STEP 2

3. **Predict** Repeat Step 2. This time, have a partner slide a sheet of paper between the magnet and the clip. Tell what you think will happen to the clip. Try it.

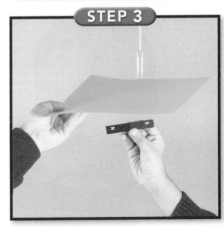
STEP 3

Think and Share

1. **Communicate** What made the paper clip move?

2. **Infer** Where does a magnet's force get weaker?

Guided Inquiry

Experiment Find out whether a magnet's force is changed by temperature. Make a plan and try it out. **Communicate** your results.

◎ **Reading Skill**

Draw Conclusions

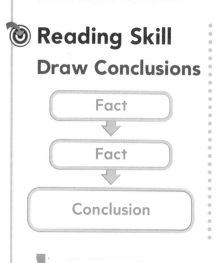

Fact

↓

Fact

↓

Conclusion

Magnets Work from a Distance

Magnetic force is the pushing or pulling force of a magnet. Magnetic force can make an object move without touching the object. Magnetic force acts on magnetic objects and also on other magnets. When like poles from two magnets are near each other, it is magnetic force that pushes the magnets away from one another.

Magnets work through paper.

Magnets work through air.

A magnet's force can attract objects through other materials. A magnet's force may work through paper, glass, plastic, water, and air. If one of these materials comes between a magnet and a magnetic object, the object may still move toward the magnet.

Magnets work through plastic.

Draw Conclusions How can a magnet hold a picture to a refrigerator?

Magnets work through glass and water.

Express Lab

Activity Card 25
Move Objects with Magnets

Weakening a Magnet's Force

Magnetic force weakens as an object is moved farther away from a magnet. This happens because the object is moving farther away from the magnetic field.

A strong magnet has a larger magnetic field. It will have a stronger force on magnetic objects. A strong magnet can attract an object from farther away.

Draw Conclusions Why won't a weak magnet work through a thick material, such as wood?

This magnet's force is very strong. It can attract the heavy toy through a thick piece of wood.

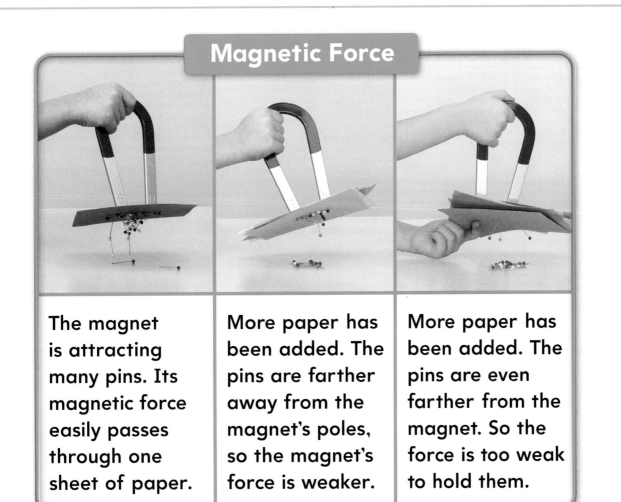

Magnetic Force

The magnet is attracting many pins. Its magnetic force easily passes through one sheet of paper.

More paper has been added. The pins are farther away from the magnet's poles, so the magnet's force is weaker.

More paper has been added. The pins are even farther from the magnet. So the force is too weak to hold them.

1. **Vocabulary** What is **magnetic force**?

2. **Reading Skill** Why might a magnet be unable to pick up a magnetic object from a distance?

3. **Predict** Could a strong magnet attract an iron object through glass? Tell why or why not.

Technology Visit **www.eduplace.com/cascp** to find out more about magnetic force.

EXTREME Science

MAGNET POWER!

What blasts this roller coaster to 112 kilometers an hour in just four seconds? Not a motor! Magnetic force does it. Magnetic coils along the track create powerful forces that rapidly pull (attract) and push (repel) the cars without touching them.

Hold on! The hidden super-powerful magnets of the V2: Vertical Velocity roller coaster at Vallejo, California, will soon rocket these riders 50 meters into the air!

My Journal

Draw your own roller coaster in your journal. Label where you would put the magnets.

Math Measure Magnetic Strength

Compare the strength of three different magnets. Place a paper clip next to a pole of a magnet. Move the clip away from the pole until the magnet no longer moves the clip. Measure and record that distance. Which magnet has the strongest force?

Magnet	Distance

Writing Describe an Event

Write a story about a time when someone used a magnet to pick something up or make something move. Tell what happened first, next, and last.

Dr. Bamidele Kammen

Meet Dr. Bamidele Kammen. She is a radiologist at Children's Hospital and Research Center in Oakland, California. A radiologist uses machines to take pictures of the inside of a person's body.

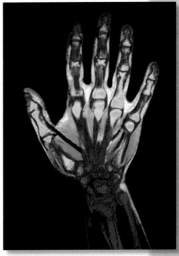

the inside of a person's hand

One of the machines uses magnets. Another machine uses X-rays. Later, Dr. Kammen looks at the pictures to see if all is well inside a person.

Visual Summary

Magnets attract objects made of iron or steel. They can make some objects move without touching them.

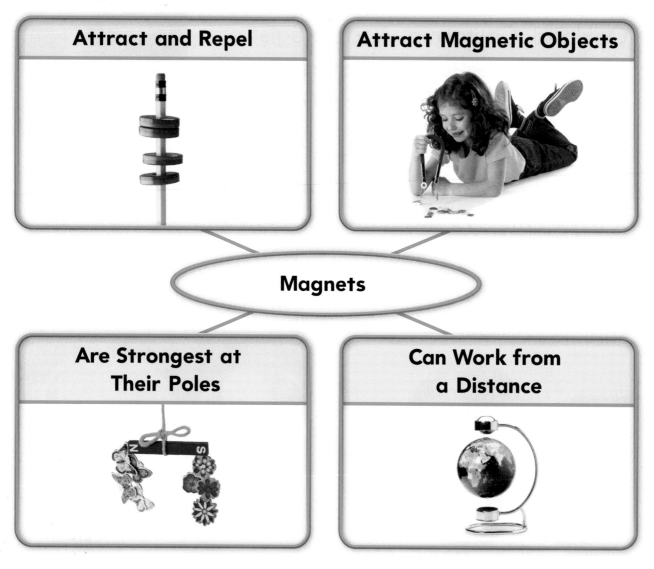

Attract and Repel

Attract Magnetic Objects

Magnets

Are Strongest at Their Poles

Can Work from a Distance

Review your answers to the Lesson Preview questions.

STANDARDS 1.f.

Main Ideas

1. What can the magnetic force of one magnet do to another magnet? **(p. 252)**

2. Where on a magnet is the force strongest? **(p. 259)**

3. What happens to magnetic force as a magnet is moved farther away from an object? **(p. 264)**

Vocabulary

Choose the correct word from the box.

4. An object that is attracted by a magnet

5. The space around a magnet where the magnet's force works

6. Pushes an object away from itself

7. To pull toward each other

attract (p. 250)
magnetic (p. 250)
repels (p. 253)
magnetic field (p. 258)

Using Science Skills

8. Predict what will happen if you put a magnet near a pile of steel paper clips.

9. **Critical Thinking** Why might a magnet be able to hold one object to a refrigerator door but not another?

STANDARDS 1–7: 1.f., 8: 4.a., 9: 1.f.

Chapter 8

Making Sound

Girl playing a violin

LESSON

1

When you pluck the strings of a harp, it makes a sound. Why does this happen?

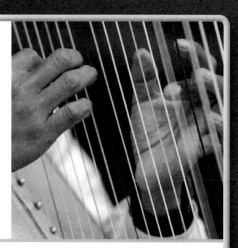

LESSON

2

A sound can have a high or a low pitch. How can you describe the pitch of these party horns?

LESSON

3

A lion makes a loud sound. How are the sounds of a lion and a kitten different?

My Journal

Write or draw in your journal to answer the questions above.

Vocabulary Preview

Vocabulary

energy p. 278

sound p. 278

vibrates p. 278

sound waves p. 280

pitch p. 286

volume p. 292

Picture Glossary
English-Spanish p. H18

Vocabulary Skill

Find All the Meanings

pitch

A word can have more than one meaning. You may already know that a **pitch** is a way of throwing a ball. The word **pitch** also is used to describe how high or low a sound is.

vibrates
Sound is made when an object vibrates, or moves back and forth quickly.

pitch
Pitch is how high or low a sound is.

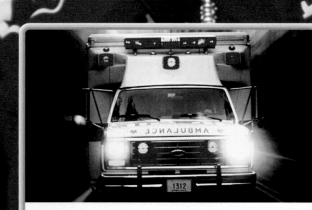

volume
Volume is how loud or soft a sound is.

Standard Set 1. Physical Sciences

1.g. *Students know* sound is made by vibrating objects and can be described by its pitch and volume.

Standard Set 4. Investigation and Experimentation covered in this chapter: 4.a., 4.d., 4.g.

sound

Sound is a form of energy that you hear.

How Is Sound Made?

Building Background

Sound is made when an object vibrates. You can observe an object vibrating.

Inquiry Skill

Work Together You can work as a team to share ideas and still think for yourself about what you observe.

▶ **STANDARDS**

1.g. *Students know* sound is made by vibrating objects and can be described by its pitch and volume.
4.d. Write or draw descriptions of a sequence of steps, events, and observations.

What You Need

goggles

plastic jar

wax paper and rubber band

pieces of paper

Making Sound

Steps

1. **Work Together** Stretch a piece of wax paper over the opening of a jar. Have a partner use a rubber band to hold the wax paper in place. **Safety:** Wear goggles!

2. Put paper pieces on the wax paper.

3. **Work Together** Gently tap the wax paper over the opening or pluck the rubber band. Talk with your partner about what you see and hear.

STEP 1

STEP 2

STEP 3

Think and Share

1. **Infer** What caused the paper to move the way it did?

2. **Predict** How could you cause the paper to move differently?

Guided Inquiry

Experiment Can you make sound with only a jar and a rubber band? Make a plan. Write each step and test your plan. **Communicate** what you observed.

277

▶ **Vocabulary**

energy

sound

vibrates

sound waves

🎯 **Reading Skill**

Cause and Effect

Cause ➡ Effect

⬛ STANDARDS

1.g. *Students know* sound is made by vibrating objects and can be described by its pitch and volume.

What Makes Sound

Energy is the ability to cause change. **Sound** is a form of energy that you hear. Sound is made when an object **vibrates**, or moves back and forth very quickly.

You can see some things vibrate. When you pluck the strings of a banjo, the strings vibrate. When you beat the head of a drum, the drumhead vibrates.

vibrating strings

vibrating drumhead

The vibrations of the strings and the drumhead make the air around them vibrate. You cannot see air vibrate. But you hear the vibrating air as sound.

A flute is shaped like a long tube. When you play a flute, you blow air across a hole in the tube. Blowing causes air inside the tube to move back and forth. As the air moves back and forth, it makes a sound.

Cause and Effect **What causes sound?**

vibrating air

Express Lab

Activity Card 26
Observe Sound

How You Hear

You use your ears to hear sound. The air vibrates. Vibrating air moves in waves called **sound waves**. Sound waves move into your ear. They make parts inside your ear vibrate. This causes a nerve in your ear to send a message to your brain. Your brain understands this message as sound.

sound waves

nerve

outer ear

vibrating parts

These are two different kinds of hearing aids.

Some people need help to hear. They use hearing aids. A hearing aid has many parts. Some parts change sound waves to make sounds louder. Other parts help move sound waves into the ear.

Cause and Effect What happens as sound waves move through the ear?

Lesson Wrap-Up

❶ **Vocabulary** What is **sound**?

❷ **Reading Skill** What causes a person to hear sounds?

❸ **Work Together** How does working with others help you decide about things?

Technology Visit www.eduplace.com/cascp to find out more about how sound is made.

STANDARDS 1–3: 1.g.

**Read these poems about sounds
made by different objects.**

Wind Song

by Lilian Moore

When the wind blows
the quiet things speak.
Some whisper, some clang,
Some creak.

Grasses swish.
Treetops sigh.
Flags slap
and snap at the sky.
Wires on poles
whistle and hum.
Ashcans roll.
Windows drum.

When the wind goes—
suddenly
then,
the quiet things
are quiet again.

STANDARDS

1.g. *Students know* sound is made by vibrating objects and can be described by its pitch and volume.

READING **LINK**

My House's Night Song

by Betsy R. Rosenthal

Listen closely.
Can you hear?

Heater whooshing out
warm air.

Blinds flapping.
Floors creaking.

Clocks ticking.
Faucet leaking.

Dishwasher clicking.
Pipes pinging.

Listen closely.
My house is singing.

TICK
TOCK
TICK

Sharing Ideas

1. **Write About It** List three objects in the poems that make sounds. Write about each sound and what caused it.

2. **Talk About It** Why do you think each poet uses the word song in the poem's title?

283

What Is Pitch?

Building Background

A pitch can be high or low. Changing the length of a vibrating object or the speed of the vibrations will change the pitch.

Inquiry Skill

Infer Instead of guessing, use what you observe and know to tell what you think.

8 straws

scissors

tape

STANDARDS

1.g. *Students know* sound is made by vibrating objects and can be described by its pitch and volume.
4.a. Make predictions based on observed patterns and not random guessing.

High or Low

Steps

① **Measure** Cut each straw to a different length.
Safety: Scissors are sharp!

STEP 1

② Put the straws in order from longest to shortest on a strip of tape. Put another strip of tape across the other side of the straws.

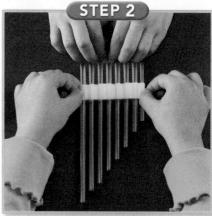

STEP 2

③ **Observe** Blow across the top of each straw. Decide which of the sounds made are high and which are low.

STEP 3

Think and Share

1. **Infer** How does the length of the straw affect the sound that the straw makes?

2. **Predict** If you blew across the end of a long paper tube, would the sound that is made be a high sound or a low sound? Why?

Guided Inquiry

Experiment Collect tubes of different sizes. **Predict** which will make the highest sound. Order the tubes from highest to lowest sound. Test your predictions.

Pitch

You can describe sound by its pitch. **Pitch** is how high or low a sound is. Something that vibrates quickly makes a sound with a high pitch. Something that vibrates slowly makes a sound with a low pitch. You can change the pitch of a sound by changing the speed at which something vibrates.

The short violin strings vibrate more quickly than the long bass strings. The violin has a higher pitch.

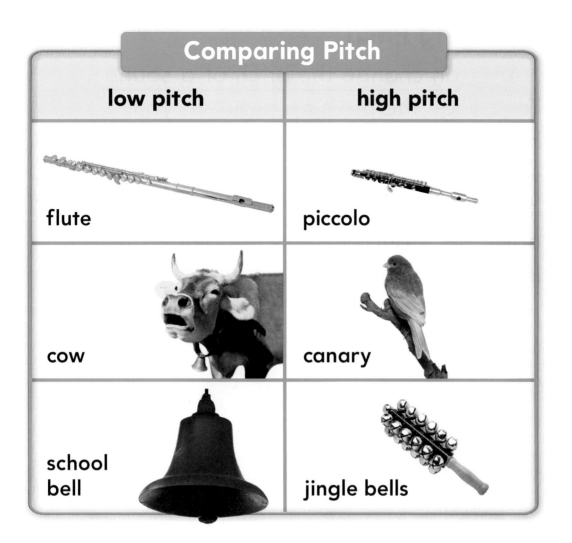

Comparing Pitch

low pitch	high pitch
flute	piccolo
cow	canary
school bell	jingle bells

An object's size also can tell about its sound. A short or small object often makes a sound with a high pitch.

Main Idea What kind of sound is made by an object that vibrates quickly?

Express Lab

Activity Card 27
Compare Sounds

Changing Pitch

You can change the pitch of a sound. To change the pitch on a guitar, you can shorten the part of the string that vibrates. You shorten the string by holding it down on the neck of the guitar. Holding down the string close to the place where it is plucked makes the string shorter.

Short strings vibrate quickly and have a higher pitch.

Long strings vibrate slowly and have a lower pitch.

In some instruments, sound is made by air vibrating inside the instrument. The length of the space where the air vibrates can be changed with a slide or with holes. Changing the length of the part that is vibrating changes the pitch.

Covering and uncovering the holes changes the pitch of this whistle.

Main Idea How can you change the pitch of an instrument?

Moving the slide on this whistle changes the length of the vibrating air inside it.

Lesson Wrap-Up

❶ **Vocabulary** What is **pitch**?

❷ **Reading Skill** What kind of sound is made by fast vibrations?

❸ **Infer** You have tall and short empty bottles. Describe the sounds that the bottles make.

Technology Visit www.eduplace.com/cascp to find out more about pitch.

What Is a Sound's Volume?

Building Background

All sounds can be loud or soft. You can make a sound louder by striking the vibrating object with more force.

Inquiry Skill

Experiment When you experiment, you choose the items you will need and plan the steps you will follow.

What You Need

goggles

rubber band

can

STANDARDS

1.g. *Students know* sound is made by vibrating objects and can be described by its pitch and volume.
4.g. Follow oral instructions for a scientific investigation.

Loud or Soft

Steps

1. **Safety:** Wear goggles. Hold the rubber band carefully! Stretch a rubber band around a can, across the open top.

2. **Experiment** Use your finger to pluck the rubber band. Try ways to make the sound louder or softer.

3. **Record Data** Write what you did differently each time and how it sounded. Use a chart like the one shown.

STEP 1

STEP 2

STEP 3

What I Did	What I Heard

Think and Share

1. **Compare** How did you change the volume?

2. Did plucking the rubber band harder affect the pitch? How do you know?

Guided Inquiry

Experiment Discuss with a group how to change the volume of sounds made by different objects. **Work together** to follow a group member's plan.

STANDARDS

1.g. *Students know* sound is made by vibrating objects and can be described by its pitch and volume.

Volume

Volume is how loud or soft a sound is. Like waves at the beach, sound waves can be big or small. Big sound waves carry a lot of energy. When sound waves are big, the sound is loud. Small sound waves carry less energy. The sound is softer.

When you whisper, you use a little energy to make a soft sound. ▼

▲ **A bike's horn is louder than a whisper and softer than a siren.**

A sound can seem to get louder as you get closer to it. The sound seems to get softer as you get farther away.

Compare and Contrast How is a big sound wave different from a small sound wave?

The sound of the space shuttle blasting off can hurt your ears. ▼

A loud siren alerts you to danger.

Express Lab

Activity Card 28
Change Volume

Comparing Pitch and Volume

You know that pitch is how high or low a sound is. You also know that volume is how loud or soft a sound is. <u>Sounds with either high or low pitches can have a loud or soft volume.</u> A foghorn has a low pitch and a loud volume. A baby pig's squeal has a high pitch and a soft volume.

A heartbeat has a low pitch and a soft volume.

A tugboat's horn has a low pitch and a loud volume.

This whistle makes a high-pitched sound with a loud volume.

This mouse makes a high-pitched sound with a soft volume.

 **Compare and Contrast** How are the sounds of a mouse and a whistle alike and different?

Lesson Wrap-Up

❶ **Vocabulary** What is **volume**?

❷ **Reading Skill** How can two sounds be alike and different?

❸ **Experiment** How is experimenting with sound useful?

Technology Visit www.eduplace.com/cascp to find out more about volume.

STANDARDS 1–3: 1.g.

A Whale of a Sound

Now hear this! If you yelled your loudest, could someone hear you a block away? Maybe. Would someone hear you a kilometer away? Not a chance!

The blue whale is the largest and the loudest animal on Earth. The sound waves it sends out are louder than the noise of a jet engine! Its bellow can be heard hundreds of kilometers away.

The smaller humpback whale sings complex songs. These songs vary in pitch from high squeals to low rumbles.

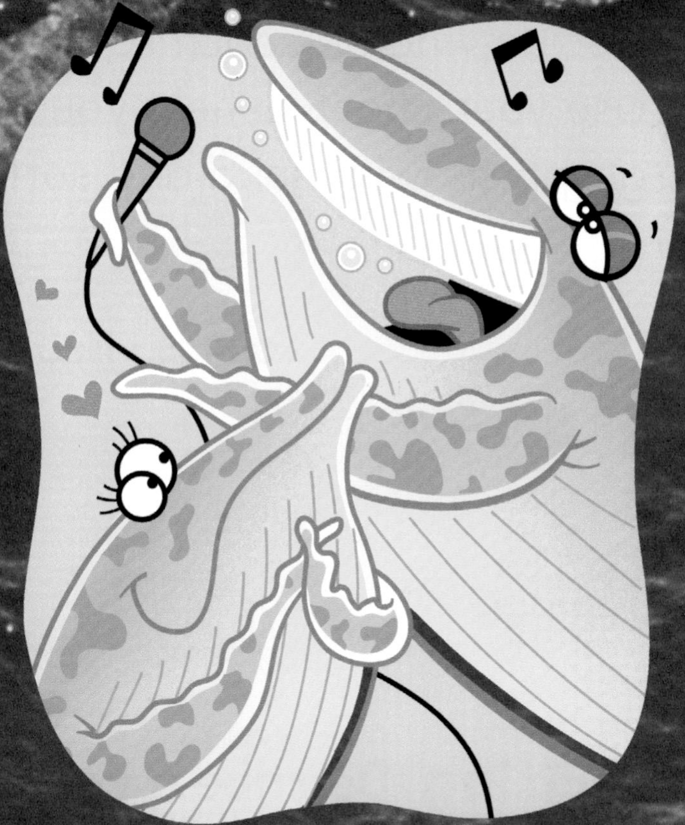

A blue whale can grow up to 30 meters long. It can weigh as much as 20 elephants!

My Journal

Can you think of any sounds louder than a blue whale? Write your ideas in your journal.

297

Math Make a Bar Graph

Make a chart like the one shown. Go to a place where you will hear many sounds. Listen for five minutes. Record each sound. Decide whether each sound is loud or soft. Use your chart to help you make a bar graph showing loud and soft sounds.

Sounds I Heard	
Sounds	Loud or Soft

Writing Describe a Person

Think of a singer, a sports announcer, or a musician. Write a paragraph that tells how the person makes sounds. Are the sounds loud or soft, high or low? Tell whether the person changes the pitch and volume of the sounds.

Sound Effects Technician

In movies and on television, all sorts of sounds help tell a story. Unusual sounds are called sound effects. The job of making them belongs to the sound effects technician.

Today, technicians usually use computers to make sound effects. But they also use many everyday objects.

What It Takes!

- Classes in computers and film
- Good listening skills

Visual Summary

Sound is made by vibrating objects. The volume of a sound can be loud or soft. The pitch of a sound can be high or low.

High Pitch

Low Pitch

Sound

Loud Volume

Soft Volume

My Journal

Review your answers to the Lesson Preview questions.

STANDARDS 1.g.

Main Ideas

1. How is sound made? (p. 278)

2. What kind of sound is made by something that vibrates very quickly? (p. 286)

3. How are big sound waves different from small sound waves? (p. 292)

Vocabulary

Choose the correct word from the box.

4. The waves that move vibrating air

5. How loud or soft a sound is

6. Something that can cause change

7. How high or low a sound is

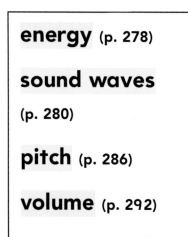

energy (p. 278)

sound waves (p. 280)

pitch (p. 286)

volume (p. 292)

Using Science Skills

8. Describe how you hear a sound. List the steps in order.

9. **Critical Thinking** Do you use more or less energy when you sing louder?

Choose the correct answer.

1. Something that a magnet attracts is _____.

   force   magnetic   pole

   ○   ○   ○

2. Unlike poles _____ each other.

   repel   push   attract

   ○   ○   ○

3. Which object is most likely nonmagnetic?

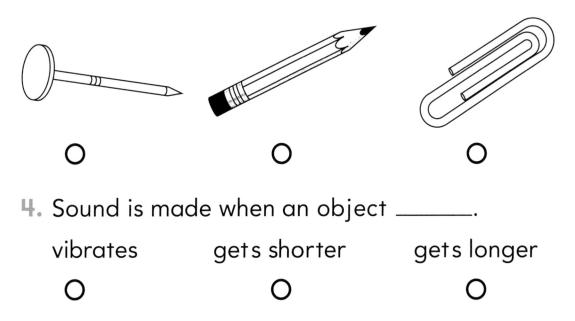

   ○   ○   ○

4. Sound is made when an object _____.

   vibrates   gets shorter   gets longer

   ○   ○   ○

5. Volume is how _____ a sound is.

loud	high	long
O	O	O

6. When you shorten the strings on a guitar, you make the pitch _____.

lower	higher	louder
O	O	O

Checking Main Ideas

Write the correct answer.

7. You move a magnet under a table and paper clips on top of the table move. Why?

8. Describe the pitch and volume of the sounds these animals make.

You Can...

Discover More

How can you hear music through a wall?

Sound travels through solids, liquids, and gases. Music can travel through a wall because a wall is a solid. The music moves out from the object that made the sound. Then it moves through the air and the wall to your ear.

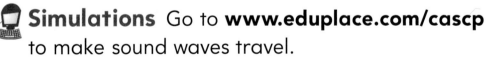 **Simulations** Go to **www.eduplace.com/cascp** to make sound waves travel.

Science and Math Toolbox

Using a Hand Lens H2

Using a Thermometer H3

Using a Ruler H4

Using a Calculator H5

Using a Balance H6

Making a Chart H7

Making a Tally Chart H8

Making a Bar Graph H9

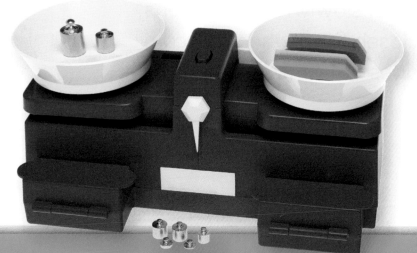

Using a Hand Lens

A hand lens is a tool that makes objects look bigger. It helps you see the small parts of an object.

Look at a Coin

1 Place a coin on your desk.

STEP 1

2 Hold the hand lens above the coin. Look through the lens. Slowly move the lens away from the coin. What do you see?

3 Keep moving the lens away until the coin looks blurry.

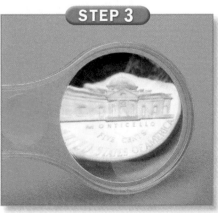
STEP 3

4 Then slowly move the lens closer. Stop when the coin does not look blurry.

STEP 4

Using a Thermometer

A thermometer is a tool used to measure temperature. Temperature tells how hot or cold something is. It is measured in degrees.

Find the Temperature of Water

 Put water into a cup.

② Put a thermometer into the cup.

③ Watch the colored liquid in the thermometer. What do you see?

④ Find the top of the red liquid. What number is next to it? That is the temperature of the water.

Using a Ruler

A ruler is a tool used to measure the length of objects. Rulers measure length in inches or centimeters.

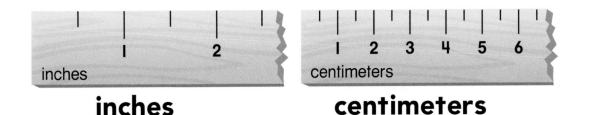

inches   **centimeters**

Measure a Crayon

1 Place the ruler on your desk.

2 Lay your crayon next to the ruler. Line up one end with the end of the ruler.

3 Look at the other end of the crayon. Which number is closest to that end?

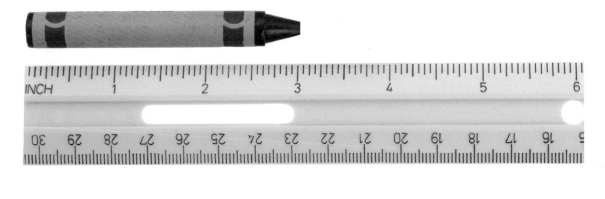

Using a Calculator

A calculator is a tool that can help you add and subtract numbers.

Subtract Numbers

1. Tim and Anna grew plants. Tim grew 5 plants. Anna grew 8 plants.

2. How many more plants did Anna grow? Use your calculator to find out.

3. Enter 8 on the calculator. Then press the − key. Enter 5 and press = .

What is your answer?

Tim's Plants

Anna's Plants

Using a Balance

A balance is a tool used to measure mass. Mass is the amount of matter in an object.

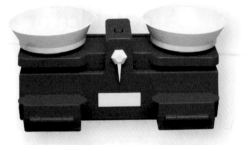

Compare the Mass of Objects

 Check that the pointer is on the middle mark of the balance. If needed, move the slider on the back to the left or right.

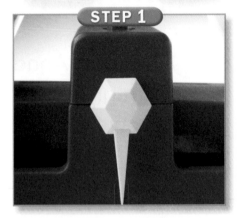
STEP 1

2 Place a clay ball in one pan. Place a crayon in the other pan.

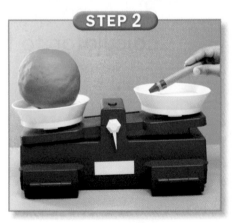
STEP 2

3 Observe the positions of the two pans.

Does the clay ball or the crayon have more mass?

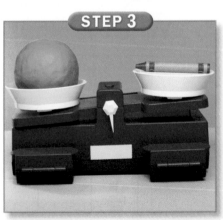
STEP 3

Making a Chart

A chart can help you sort information, or data. When you sort data it is easier to read and compare.

Make a Chart to Compare Animals

1 Give the chart a title.

2 Name the groups that tell about the data you collect. Label the columns with the names.

3 Carefully fill in the data in each column.

Which animal can move in the most ways?

How Animals Move	
Animal	How it Moves
fish	swim
dog	walk, swim
duck	walk, fly, swim

Making a Tally Chart

A tally chart helps you keep track of items as you count.

Make a Tally Chart of Kinds of Pets

Jan's class made a tally chart to record the number of each kind of pet they own.

1. Every time they counted one pet, they made one tally.

2. When they got to five, they made the fifth tally a line across the other four.

3. Count the tallies to find each total.

How many of each kind of pet do the children have?

Kinds of Pets

Kinds of Pets	
cat	卌 ‖
dog	卌 ‖‖
hamster	‖‖

Making a Bar Graph

A bar graph can help you sort and compare data.

Make a Bar Graph of Favorite Pets

You can use the data in the tally chart on page H8 to make a bar graph.

 Choose a title for your graph.

 Write numbers along the side.

 Write pet names along the bottom.

 Start at the bottom of each column. Fill in one box for each tally.

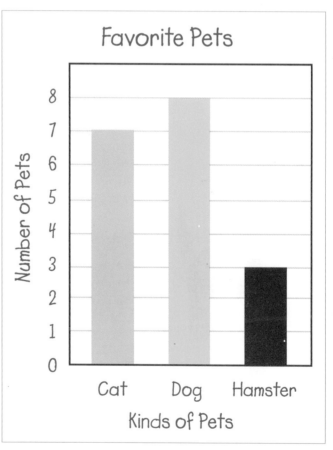

Favorite Pets

Number of Pets

Cat   Dog   Hamster

Kinds of Pets

Which pet is the favorite?

Health and Fitness Handbook

When your body works well, you are healthy. Here are some ways to stay healthy.

- Know how your body works.

- Follow safety rules.

- Dance, jump, run, or swim to make your body stronger.

- Eat foods that give your body what it needs.

Your Senses.................................H12
Your senses tell you about the
world around you.

Protect Eyes and Ears.....................H14
Learn how to protect your
eyes and ears.

Staying Safe on the Road H15
Be safe when you walk or when
you ride in a car or bus.

Move Your Muscles! H16
There are many ways to
exercise your muscles.

Food Groups.....................................H17
Eat foods from different
groups.

Your Senses

Your five senses help you learn about the world. They help you stay safe.

Sight

Light enters the eye through the pupil. The iris controls how much light comes in. Other parts of the eye turn the light into messages that go to the brain.

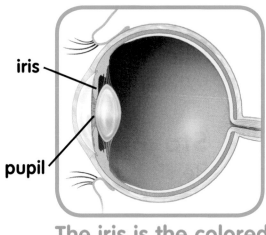

iris

pupil

The iris is the colored part of the eye.

Hearing

The ear has three main parts. Most of your ear is inside your head. Sound makes some parts of the ear move back and forth very fast. The inner ear sends information about the sound to the brain.

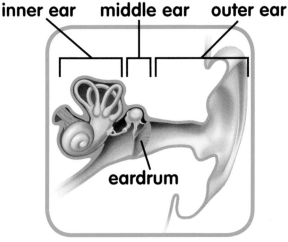

inner ear   middle ear   outer ear

eardrum

The eardrum is easily injured. Never stick anything in your ear.

Taste

Your tongue is covered with thousands of tiny bumps called taste buds. They help you taste sweet, salty, sour, and bitter things. Some parts of the tongue seem to sense some flavors more strongly. The whole tongue tastes salty foods.

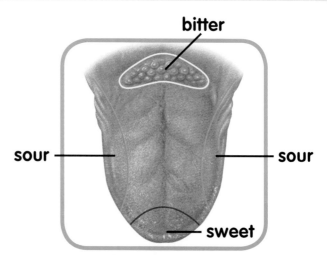

bitter

sour — — sour

sweet

Your body makes a new set of taste buds about every two weeks.

Smell

All kinds of smells travel through the air. These smells enter your nose. Your nose sends messages to your brain about them.

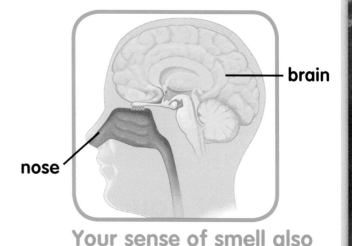

brain

nose

Your sense of smell also helps you taste.

Touch

Touch a tree trunk, and it feels rough. A kitten feels soft. Your skin senses all this information. Then the brain decides how to respond.

Your skin is your body's largest organ.

Protect Eyes and Ears

You use your eyes and ears to see and hear. You can protect your eyes and ears.

Protect Your Eyes

- Keep sharp things away from your eyes.

- Wear sunglasses when you are outside. They protect your eyes from the Sun's rays.

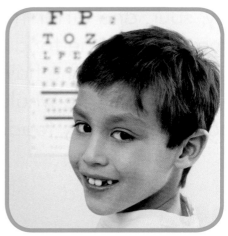

An eye test can help tell if a person needs glasses.

Protect Your Ears

- Wear a helmet when you play baseball or softball.

- Loud noises can damage your ears. Keep music at a low volume.

A hearing test tells if a person has a hearing loss.

Staying Safe on the Road

How do you get to school or a playground? Here are ways to help you stay safe.

Walk Safely

- Stay on the sidewalk.

- Walk with a friend or trusted adult.

- Cross at crosswalks. Look both ways before you cross!

- Don't run between parked cars. Drivers might not see you.

Car and Bus Safety

- If a bus has seat belts, wear one.

- Stay seated and talk quietly so the driver can pay attention to the road.

- Cross the street in front of a bus after all traffic stops.

Only cross when the "walk" sign is lit.

Obey crossing guards.

Always wear your seat belt in a car.

Move Your Muscles!

All kinds of things can be exercise. Here are some ways you can make your muscles stronger.

By Yourself

- Kick a ball as far as you can. Chase it and kick it back.
- Ride your bike.
- Jump rope.
- Do jumping jacks.
- Put on music and dance.

With Others

- Play ball!
- Play tag. Run!
- Go for a hike.
- Play hopscotch.
- Play with a flying disk.

Food Groups

Food gives your body energy and what your body needs to grow. Foods in different groups help you in different ways.

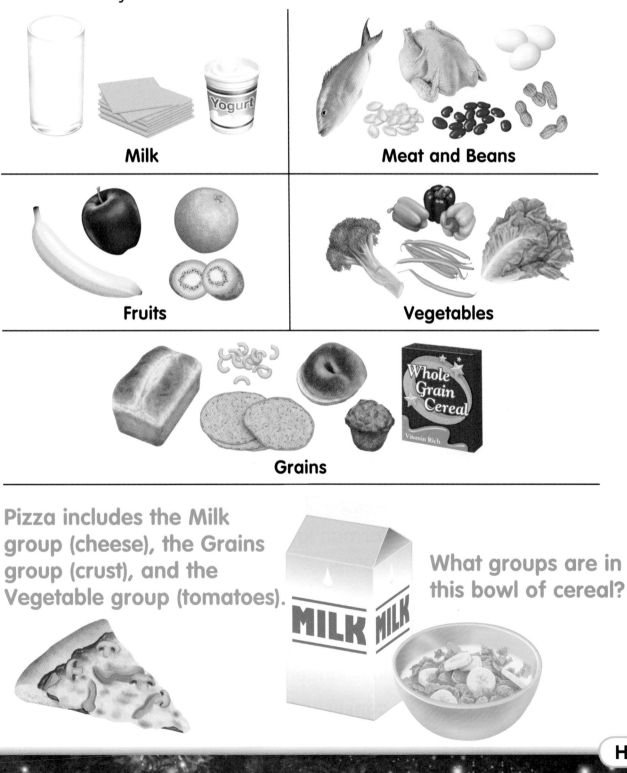

Milk

Meat and Beans

Fruits

Vegetables

Grains

Pizza includes the Milk group (cheese), the Grains group (crust), and the Vegetable group (tomatoes).

What groups are in this bowl of cereal?

MILK MILK

English-Spanish

Picture Glossary

A

adult
An animal that is full grown. (49)
adulto Animal que se ha desarrollado totalmente.

attract
When objects pull toward each other. (250)
atraer Cuando los objetos empujan hacia sí a otros objetos.

C

cone
The part of a plant where seeds form in plants without flowers. (14)
cono Parte de la planta donde se forman las semillas de plantas sin flores.

conserve
To use less of something to make it last longer. (156)
conservar Usar algo poco a poco para que dure más.

D

direction

The path that an object follows. (212)

dirección Recorrido que sigue un objeto.

distance

The length of space between two people, places, or things. (180)

distancia El espacio que hay entre dos personas, lugares o cosas.

E

energy

The ability to cause change. (206, 278)

energía La capacidad de causar cambios.

environment

All the living and nonliving things around a living thing. (27)

medio ambiente Todos los seres vivos y las cosas sin vida que rodean a un ser vivo.

erosion

The carrying of weathered rock and soil from place to place. (100)

erosión El desgaste y movimiento de roca y tierra.

F

fertile

Soil that is full of the nutrients needed to grow plants. (148)

fértil Suelo que está lleno de los nutrientes que las plantas necesitan para crecer.

flower

The part of a plant where fruit and seeds form. (10)

flor Parte de la planta donde se forma la fruta y las semillas.

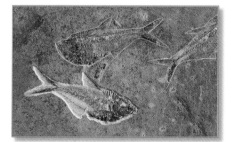

force

A push or a pull. (204)

fuerza Movimiento que empuja o atrae.

fossil

Something that remains of a living thing from long ago. (114)

fósil Lo que queda de un ser vivo que existió hace mucho tiempo.

friction

A force that makes an object slow down when it rubs against another object. (208)

fricción Fuerza que hace que un objeto pierda velocidad cuando roza contra otro.

fruit

The part of a flower that is around a seed. (10)

fruta Parte de la flor que está alrededor de la semilla.

fuel

A material that is burned to provide power or heat. (132)

combustible Materia que se puede quemar para obtener energía o calor.

gravity

A force that causes objects to fall to the ground unless something holds them up. (34, 100, 230)

gravedad hace que los objetos caigan al suelo a menos que algo los sostenga.

humus

Tiny bits of dead plants and animals in soil. (104)

humus Trocitos pequeños de plantas y

I

individual

One living thing in a group of the same kind of living things. (69)

individuo Ser vivo que pertenece a un grupo del mismo tipo de seres vivos.

inherit

To have traits passed on from the parent. (20)

heredar Tener rasgos que provienen del progenitor.

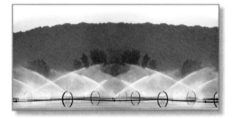

irrigation

A way to bring water to dry land. (144)

riego Método para llevar agua a la tierra seca.

L

larva

The worm-like stage in an insect's life cycle. (56)

larva En el ciclo de vida de un insecto, fase en la que es similar a un gusano.

learned

Traits that are not passed on from parents to their offspring. (62)

aprendido Rasgos que no pasan de los progenitores a la descendencia.

life cycle
The series of changes that a living thing goes through as it grows. (12)

ciclo de vida Serie de cambios por los que pasa un ser vivo al crecer.

magnet

An object that attracts iron or steel objects. (250)

imán Objeto que atrae a otros objetos de hierro y acero.

magnetic

An object that is attracted by a magnet. (250)

magnético Objeto que es atraído por un imán.

magnetic field
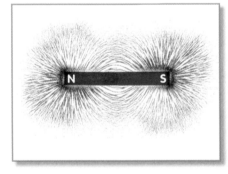

The space around a magnet where the magnet's force works. (258)

campo magnético Espacio alrededor de un imán donde actúa la fuerza magnética del imán.

magnetic force

The pushing or pulling force of a magnet. (262)

fuerza magnética La fuerza de repulsión o atracción de un imán.

mineral
A solid found in nature that was never living. (90)

mineral Sólido que se encuentra en la naturaleza y que nunca estuvo vivo.

motion
Movement from one place to another. (186)

movimiento Cambio de posición de un lugar a otro.

natural resource
Something found in nature that people need or use. (132)

recurso natural Elemento que se encuentra en la naturaleza y que la gente usa o necesita.

nutrients
Materials in soil that help a plant grow well. (104)

nutrientes Materiales del suelo que les sirven a las plantas para crecer.

O

offspring

The living things that come from a living thing. (48)

descendencia Seres vivos que descienden de otro ser vivo.

P

pitch

How high or low a sound is. (286)

tono Lo grave o agudo que es un sonido.

poles

The places on a magnet where the forces are strongest. (252)

polos Lugares de un imán donde su fuerza es mayor.

population

A group of the same kind of living thing in one place. (28)

población Grupo del mismo tipo de seres vivos que habitan un lugar.

position

A place or location. The globe is on the desk. (178)

posición Lugar o situación. El globo terráqueo está sobre el escritorio.

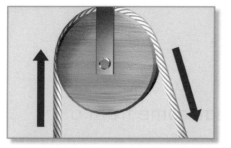

pulley
A wheel with a groove through which a rope or chain moves. (223)

polea Rueda con un canal por el que se mueve una cuerda o cadena.

pupa
The stage when an insect changes form. (56)

crisálida Fase en la que un insecto cambia de forma.

R

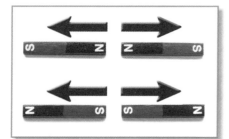

recycle
To collect items made of materials that can be used again to make new items. (158)

reciclar Acumular objetos cuyo material se puede usar otra vez para hacer nuevos objetos.

repels
When a magnet pushes an object away from itself. (253)

repeler Cuando un imán rechaza a otro objeto.

reproduce
When living things make more living things of the same kind. (48)

reproducir Cuando los seres vivos crean más seres vivos del mismo tipo.

rock

A solid made of one or more minerals. (90)

roca Sólido compuesto de uno o más minerales.

seed

The part of a plant from which a new plant grows. (10)

semilla En una planta, parte de la cual nace una nueva planta.

soil

The loose material that covers Earth's surface. (104)

tierra Material suelto que cubre la superficie de la Tierra.

sound

A form of energy that you hear. (278)

sonido Forma de energía que se puede oír.

sound waves

The waves that move vibrating air. (280)

ondas sonoras Las ondas que mueve el aire al vibrar.

speed
The distance an object moves in a set amount of time. (190)

velocidad La distancia a la que se mueve un objeto en un tiempo determinado.

vibrates
When an object moves back and forth very quickly. (278)

vibrar Cuando un objeto se mueve hacia adelante y hacia atrás muy deprisa.

volume
How loud or soft a sound is. (292)

volumen Lo alto o bajo que es un sonido.

weathering
The wearing away and breaking apart of rock. (98)

desgaste Desgaste y desprendimiento de una roca.

weight
A measure of the pull of gravity on an object. (232)

peso Medida de la fuerza de gravedad sobre un objeto.

Index

A

Adults, 44, 48–51, 54–55, 57
Air, 104, 106, 108
Airplanes, S19
Air pollution, S19
Alpaca fibers, 72–73
Amphibians, Unit A Tab, 54–55
Animals
  alike and different, 43, 66–71
  amphibians, Unit A Tab, 54–55
  birds, 48, 50–51, 64–65, Unit B Tab
  fibers from, 72–73
  fish, 48
  food for, 153
  fossils of, 85, 86, 112, 114–121, 122, 124
  inherited traits, 60–61
  insects, 16–17, 56–57, 110–111
  learned traits, 44, 62–63
  life cycles, 1, 43, 46–57
  mammals, 48, 50–51
  of Red Rock Canyon, Unit B Tab
  reptiles, S12–S13, 48, Unit B Tab
  of Sequoia National Park, Unit A Tab
  sea lions, 1, 80
  soil and, 108–109
  whales, 296–297
Animator, 195
Ask questions, S12, S14, S16
Astronauts, S10–S11, 235

B

Balance (tool), H6
Bar graph, making a, H9
Birds
  chicken feathers, 64–65
  life cycle, 50–51
  loggershead shrikes, Unit B Tab
  offspring, 48
Blue whale, 296–297
Bones, 115, 116, 117, 118
Botanist, 39
Brain, 280, H12, H13
Brakes, 215
Bus safety, H15
Butterflies, 56–57

C

Cactus, 148
Calculator, H5
Caldeiro, Fernando, S10–S11
California
  astronauts from, 235
  farming in, 144
  Hoover Dam power for, 145
  maglev trains, 254–255
  motion at the California Speedway, 216–219
  rocks in, 91
  saber-toothed cat fossils, 120–121
  sea lions, 1, 80
  seedless grapes of, 30–31
  soils and plants of, 149

Attracts, 246, 248, 250, 252–253, 255, 258–259, 260–265, 266, 270

  Vertical Velocity roller coaster, 266–267
California Big Ideas, 1, 81, 169, 241
California Field Trips
  Mariachi Festival, Unit D Tab
  Red Rock Canyon, Unit B Tab
  Sequoia National Park, Unit A Tab
  Spirit of Sacramento, Unit C Tab
California newts, Unit A Tab
California Standards, S1–S8, 7, 45, 87, 129, 175, 201, 247, 275
Careers in Science
  animator, 195
  botanist, 39
  geologist, 123
  sound effects technician, 299
Cars, 192–193
Car safety, H15
Casts, 114–115, 116
Charts, H7–H8
Chuckwalla lizard, Unit B Tab
Coal, 132, 133
Color
  of minerals, 93
  of rocks, 85, 94
  of soils, 106–107
Cones, 6, 14
Conserve, 128, 154–159, 164
Crickets, S14–S15
Critical thinking, S13
Cryobot, S18–S19

D

Dahlgren, Dr. Randy, 163
Dams, 145

Data, sorting, H7, H9
Decision making, S22–S23
Dinosaurs, 116–117, 118
Directed Inquiry
    change direction, 211
    change motion, 203
    changing rocks, 97
    compare fossils, 113
    compare life cycles, 47
    compare pea pods, 25
    compare rocks, 89
    compare soils, 103
    falling objects, 229
    filing patterns, 257
    fruits and seeds, 9
    high or low, 285
    locate an object, 177
    look for rocks, 131
    loud or soft, 291
    making sound, 277
    measure handspans, 67
    objects in motion, 185
    observe force, 261
    plant seeds, 19
    sprouting seeds, 33
    test magnets, 249
    tools push and pull, 221
    train goldfish, 59
    triops stages, 53
    wasted water, 155
    water in soil, 147
    water use, 141
Direction
    changes in, 199, 210–213, 236
    of forces, 223
Distance, 174, 180–181
    magnetic force and, 260, 262, 264–265, 270
    volume of sound and, 293
Draw conclusions, S15, S16

Eardrum, H12
Ears, 280–281, H12, H14
Earth
    changes in surface of, 96–101
    clues to past, 112–119
    gravity of, 228–233
    materials in, 81, 90, 123, 124
    study of, 123
Electricity, 145, 164
Energy
    electrical, 145, 164
    from food, H17
    forces and, 206–207
    sound, 275, 278–281, 292
Environment, 7
    animals and, 58
    clues to past, 112–119
    plants and, 27–29, 32–37, 40
Erosion, 100–101
Exercise, H16
Experiment, S14, S16, S17
Express Labs
    categorize water uses, 143
    change an object's direction, 212
    change volume, 293
    classify soil, 149
    compare leaf size, 27
    compare soils, 106
    compare sounds, 287
    compare temperature, 35
    compare two individuals, 69
    compare young plants to their parents, 21
    describe an object's location, 179

    experiment with gravity, 230
    group fossils, 117
    group rocks, 91
    identify rock uses, 132
    make a machine, 223
    match animals, 49
    measure how a frog changes, 55
    measure motion, 207
    model water waste, 156
    move objects with magnets, 263
    observe a ball's motion, 187
    observe a learned behavior, 61
    observe a magnetic field, 258
    observe how rocks change, 98
    observe magnets, 251
    observe sound, 279
    order a plant life cycle, 11
Extreme Science
    Check Out These Chickens, 64–65
    Fast, Faster, Fastest! 192–193
    Magnet Power! 266–267
    Mega Mover, 226–227
    Mighty Mite, 110–111
    Trash Bird, 160–161
    A Whale of a Sound, 296–297
    What's the Big Stink? 16–17
Eyes, H12, H14

Facts, S13
Farming, 144

Feathers, 64–65
Feldspar, 95
Fertile soil, 148
Fish, 48
Flowers, 6, 8, 10–11, 13, 16–17
Food, 71, 151, 153
Food groups, H17
Footprints, 116–117
Forces, Unit C Tab, 200
    change in direction, 210–213, 236
    change in speed, 210, 214–215, 236
    friction, 200, 208–209, 214–215
    gravity, 228–233, 236
    magnetism, 252–253, 254–255, 256–259, 260–265, 266-267, 270
    motion and, 199, 202–209, 236
    sound and, 290
    tools and machines and, 220–225, 236
Form an idea, S14, S16
Fossils, 85, 86, 112–119, 122
    clues to the past, 116–119, 122, 124
    formation of, 114–115
    of saber-toothed cats, 120–121
French, Lloyd, S18
Friction, 200, 208–209, 214
Frogs, 54–55
Fruit, 5, 8–11, 13, 22–23
    as food, 151, 152–153
Fuel, 132, 151, 156, 159, 164

Garbage, 160–161
Geologist, 123

Gills, 55
Glaciers, 100
Glass, 159, 168
Granite, 95, 133
Graphs, H9
Gravity, S11, 201, 228–233, 236
    erosion and, 100
    plants and, 34
    in space, 235
Guided Inquiry, 9, 19, 25, 33, 47, 53, 59, 67, 89, 97, 103, 113, 131, 141, 147, 155, 177, 185, 203, 211, 221, 229, 249, 257, 261, 277, 285, 291

Hand lens, H2
Hardness, 92, 94
Health and fitness, H10
    exercise, H16
    food groups, H17
    protecting eyes and ears, H14
    road safety, H15
    senses, H12–H13
Hearing, 280–281, H12
Hearing aids, 281
Heat, 132, 133, 151
History of Science
    Fossils of Saber-Toothed Cats, 120–121
    Measuring Tools Then and Now, 182–183
Hoover Dam, 145
Humpback whale, 297
Humus, 104–107, 110, 148

Imprints, 114–116
Individuals, 69

Information, collecting, S11
Inherited traits, 18–23, 40, 58, 60–61, 64–65, 68–69, 76
Inner ear, H12
Inquiry process, S14–S15
Inquiry Skills
    ask questions, 220
    classify, 46, 112
    communicate, 130
    compare, 18, 102
    experiment, 228, 290
    infer, 96, 256, 284
    measure, 66, 88, 176, 202
    observe, 8, 248
    predict, 58, 210, 260
    record data, 32, 140
    use data, 52
    use models, 154
    use numbers, 24, 146
    work together, 184, 276
Insects, 16–17, 56–57
Inventors, S18–S21
Investigations, S11–S13
Iris, H12
Iron, 248, 250, 256–259
Irrigation, 129, 144

Jeffery shooting star, Unit A Tab
Jets, S10–S11

Kammen, Dr. Bamidele, 269

Labeling charts, H7
La Brea Tar Pits, 120–121
Larva, 44, 56
Learned traits, 44, 58, 62–63, 76
Leaves, 13, 34
Levitate, 254
Life cycles
    of amphibians, 54–55
    of animals, 48–57
    of insects, 56–57
    of mammals, birds, reptiles, and fish, 46–51
    of plants, 12–15
Light, 35, H12
Links for Home and School
    math, 38, 74, 122, 162, 194, 234, 268, 298
    writing, 38, 74, 122, 162, 194, 234, 268, 298
Literature
    "Caterpillar," 2–3
    "My House's Night Song," 283
    "The Steam Shovel," 170–171
    "Wind Song," 282
Litter, S22–S23
Living things
    change over time, 112–119
    environment and, 7
    fossils of, 85, 86, 112–119
    inherited traits, 20–23
    learned traits, 44, 58, 62–63, 76
    like parents, 43, 46–51, 76
    needs of, 142
    offspring of, 18–23, 43, 46–57, 60, 76
    parents care of, 80

See also Animals; Plants.
Lizards, S12–S13, Unit B Tab
Location, 173, 174, 176–181
Loggershead shrikes, Unit B Tab
Lungs, 55
Luster, 93

Machines, 226–227
    forces and, 220–225, 236
    pulley, 223
Magnetic fields, 245, 246, 256–259, 264
Magnetic force, 260–265, 270
Magnetic objects, 247, 248, 250
Magnets, 241–271
    force of, 260–265, 270
    maglev trains, 254–255
    magnetic field, 245, 246, 256–259, 264
    on roller coaster, 266–267
Making decisions, S22–S23
Mammals, 48, 50–51
Mariachi Festival, Unit D Tab
Mass, 232–233, H6
Math Links, 16–17, 38, 74, 122, 160–161, 162, 182–183, 192–193, 194, 226–227, 234, 268, 296–297, 298
Measuring
    distance, 67, 177, 180–184, 203
    height, 19
    length, 25, 53, 113, 122, H4

mass, 89, H6
    motion, 188
    temperature, H3
    tools for, S19, 182–183
    volume, 147, 155
Meter stick, 180, 183
Metric system, 182–183
Mica, 95
Microscopes, S19
Middle ear, H12
Minerals, 86, 90–95
    properties of, 88, 92–93
    in rocks, 88, 90, 94–95
    uses for, 134–135
Motion, 169, 175
    description of, 184–189
    forces and, 199, 202–209
    magnets and, 245, 250, 252, 254–255, 266–267
    speed and, 188–191
Music, 82–83, Unit D Tab, 242–243
My Journal, 5, 17, 40, 43, 65, 76, 85, 111, 124, 127, 161, 164, 173, 193, 196, 199, 227, 236, 245, 267, 270, 273, 297, 300

Natural resources, 128
    conservation of, 154–159, 160–161
    plants, 151–153, 164
    rocks, 132–135, 164
    soil, 132, 146–150, 164
    trees, 150, 151
    water, 132, 140–145, 164
Nonmagnetic objects, 251
Nose, H13
Nutrients, 104, 109, 148

Index

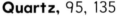

O

Objects
change in direction, 210–213
change in speed, 200, 210, 214–215
forces and, 202–209
friction and, 200, 208–209, 214
gravity and, 228–233
location of, 176–181, 196
magnetism and, 247
in motion, 169, 175, 184–191, 196, 200, 202–209
speed of, 188–191
Observe, S11, S13, S14, S16
Ocean waves, 101
Ochoa, Dr. Ellen, 235
Offspring, 18–23, 46–57, 60
environment and, 27–29, 71
inherited traits, 18–23, 40, 58, 60–61, 64–65, 68–71, 76
learned traits, 44, 58, 62–63, 76
like parents, 43, 46–51, 76
parents care of, 80
of plants, 18–23, 24–26
unlike parents, 52–57, 76
Opinions, S13
Outer ear, H12

P

Parents
caring for offspring, 80
like offspring of, 43, 46–51, 76

new plants and, 18–23
traits passed to offspring, 18–23, 40, 58, 60–61, 64–65, 68–69, 76
unlike offspring of, 54–57, 76
People
fastest runners, 240
health and fitness, H10
offspring of, 61
senses, H12–H13
use of water, 142–143
People in Science
Dahlgren, Dr. Randy, 163
Kammen, Dr. Bamidele, 269
Ochoa, Dr. Ellen, 235
Wack, Dr. Ray, 75
Pine tree, 14–15
Pitch, 273, 274, 284–289, 294–295
Plants
of California, 149
differences in same kind, 5, 24–29, 40
environment and, 7, 27–29, 32–37, 40
fossils of, 112, 114–118, 124
insect attraction, 16–17
life cycle of, 1, 12–15
needs of, 144, 148
parents and new plants, 18–23, 40
parts of, 8–11, 14
recycling and, 159
rock weathering by, 98–99
seedless grapes, 30–31
of Sequoia National Park, Unit A Tab
soil and, 102, 109, 127, 148
uses for, 146, 151–153, 164
Plastic litter, S22–S23

Poems
"Caterpillar," 2–3
"My House's Night Song," 283
"The Steam Shovel," 170–171
"Wind Song," 282
Poles of magnets, 246, 252–253, 258–259, 262, 270
Pollination, 16
Population, 6, 28–29, 70–71
Position, 173, 174, 196
description of, 176–181
motion and, 184–191, 204–207
Properties, 81
of minerals, 92–93
of rocks, 88–89, 94–95
of soils, 106–108, 148–149
Pulley, 200, 223
Pupa, 44, 56–57
Pupil, H12

Q

Quartz, 95, 135

R

Radiologist, 269
Rain, 36, 37
Readers' Theater
Motion at the California Speedway, 216–219
Rock Stars, 136–139
Reading in Science
"Caterpillar," 2–3
"Magnets," 242–243
"Rocks, Soil, and Fossils," 82–83
"The Steam Shovel," 170–171

Reading Links, 30–31, 64–65, 72–73, 110–111, 120–121, 136–139, 216–219, 254–255, 266–267, 282–283

Reading Skills
cause and effect, 34, 35, 37, 98, 100, 204, 205, 207, 208, 250, 251, 253, 278, 279, 281
classify, 90, 91, 93, 94, 142, 143, 145, 148, 151, 153
compare and contrast, 26, 27, 29, 48, 49, 50, 104, 105, 106, 109, 186, 187, 189, 191, 258, 259, 292, 293, 295
draw conclusions, 20, 21, 23, 60, 61, 63, 114, 115, 116, 119, 156, 159, 178, 180, 230, 231, 233, 262, 263, 264
main idea and details, 68, 69, 71, 132, 134, 222, 223, 224, 286, 287, 289
sequence, 10, 11, 13, 14, 54, 55, 57, 212, 214

Recycling, 127, 128, 158–159, 160–161

Red Rock Canyon, Unit B Tab

Repels, 246, 252–253, 255, 258, 262, 266-267, 270

Reproduce, 44, 45, 48, 60

Reptiles, S12–S13, Unit B Tab, 48

Resources, 81, 128
conservation of, 154–159, 160–161
plants, 151–153, 164

recycling of, 127, 128, 158
rocks, 132–135, 164
soil, 132, 146–150, 164
trees, 150, 151
water, 127, 132, 140–145, 164

Robots, S18–S19

Rocks, 86, 88–89, 90–91
changes in, 96–101
minerals in, 88, 92–93, 95, 124
properties of, 85, 88–89, 94–95
of Red Rock Canyon, Unit B Tab
sizes of, 85
in soil, 102, 104, 105, 106–107, 108
uses for, 127, 130–135, 136–139, 164, 168
weathering, 87, 124

Roots, 34

Ruler, 180, H4

Saber-toothed cat fossils, 120–121

Safety, S24, H14, H15
with eyes, H14

Sand, 132, 159

Science inquiry, S14–S15

Scientists
how they think, S12–S15
tools of, S19
what they do, S10–S11

Scooters, S20

Sea lions, 1, 80

Seat belts, H15

Seeds, 5, 6, 8–15, 18–20, 22–23

Sequoia National Park, Unit A Tab

Sight, H12

Simulators, S11

Size, 286–289, 292

Skin, H13

Smell, H13

Soil, 85, 86, 98, 110, 124
animals and, 108–109
kinds of, 106–107
materials in, 102–107, 124, 147
plants and, 127, 148–149
pollution of, 163
uses of, 146–151, 164

Soil mites, 110–111

Soil scientists, 163

Songs
"Magnets," 242–243
"Rocks, Soil, and Fossils," 82–83
of whales, 297

Sound, 273, 275, 276–281, 292, 304, H12
pitch, 273, 274, 284–289, 294–295, 300
sound effects technician, 299
volume, 273, 274, 290–295, 300
of whales, 296–297

Sound effects technician, 299

Sound waves, 280–281, 292

Space, 29

Space shuttle, S10–S11

Speed, 173, 174, 184, 188–191
changes in, 210, 214–215, 236
friction and, 200, 208–209, 214–215
of vibrations, 286

Spirit of Sacramento, Unit C Tab

Stems, 13, 34, 35

Sunlight, 35

Surfaces, 208–209

Index

Tally chart, H8
Taste, H13
Taste buds, H13
Technology, S19
  Great Grapes, 30–31
  Maglev Trains, 254–255
  Spin a Yarn, 72–73
Temperature
  crickets and, S14–S15
  lizards and, S13
  measuring, H3
  plants and, 36, 37
Thermometer, H3
Thompson, George, 30
Thompson, William, 30
Titan arum, 16–17
Tongue, H13
Tools of scientists
  balance, H6
  calculator, H5
  forces and, 199, 236
  hand lens, H2
  for measuring distance,
    182–183
  microscope, S19
  pulley, 223
  robots, S18–S19
  ruler, H4
  technology, S19
  thermometer, H3
  work and, 220–225
Touch, 34, 35, H13
Traits
  environment and, 27–
    29

inherited, 18–23, 26, 40,
  58, 60–61, 64–65, 76
learned, 44, 58, 62–63,
  76
of new plants from
  same parents, 24–26
Trash, 160–161
Trees
  with cones, 14–15
  conservation of, 159
  with flowers, 11
  inherited traits, 22–23
  life cycle of, 14–15
  as natural resource,
    150, 151
  sequoia, Unit A Tab
  wind and, 36
Tyrannosaurus rex, 116–
  117

Veterinarian, 75
Vibrating, 274, 276–281,
  300
  pitch and, 284–289
Vocabulary Skills
  find all the meanings,
    200, 274
  use opposites, 246
  use pictures, 128
  use syllables, 6, 86
  use what's before, 44
  use words, 174
Volume, 273, 274, 290–
  295
Vomit comet, S11

Wack, Dr. Ray, 75
Walking safely, H15
Water
  conservation of, 156,
    157, 159
  erosion by, 100–101
  as natural resource,
    142–145
  plants and, 29, 37
  rock weathering by, 96,
    98–99
  in soil, 104, 106, 108,
    147, 148
  uses for, 127, 140–145,
    164
Waves, 101, 280–281
Weather, 36
Weathering, 87, 98–99,
  124
Weight, 232–233
Whales, 296–297
Wind
  erosion by, 100, 101
  plants and, 36
  rock weathering by, 96,
    98–99
Work, 200, 220–225
Work together, S11, S12,
  184, 276
Writing Links, 38, 74,
  122, 162, 194, 234, 268,
  298

Permission Acknowledgements

Caterpillar by Mary Dawson. Copyright © Mary Dawson. Our best efforts have been made to locate the rights holder of this selection. If anyone has any information as to the whereabouts of the author or her representatives, please contact the School Permissions Department at Houghton Mifflin Company, 222 Berkeley Street, Boston, MA 02116. Excerpt from *My House's Night Song* from *My House is Singing*, by Betsy R. Rosenthal. Copyright © 2004 by Betsy R. Rosenthal. Reprinted by permission of Harcourt, Inc. *The Steam Shovel*, by Rowena Bennett. Copyright © 1948 by Rowena Bennett. Reprinted by permission of Kenneth C. Bennett. *Wind Song* from *I Feel The Same Way*, by Lilian Moore. Copyright © 1967, 1995 by Lilian Moore. Reprinted by permission of Marian Reiner Literary Agency.

Cover and Title Page

Front cover (Garibaldi) © Gregory Ochocki/Photo Researchers, Inc. (water background) © Flip Nicklin/Minden Pictures.Back cover © Flip Nicklin/Minden Pictures. Spine © Gregory Ochocki/Photo Researchers, Inc. Title page © Gregory Ochocki/Photo Researchers, Inc. End Paper (t) Brandon D. Cole/Corbis. (b) © 1994 M.C. Chamberlain/DRK Photo.

Photography

iv Robert Lubeck/Animals Animals. v Dr. John Cunningham/Visuals Unlimited. vi © NHPA/Daniel Heuclin. vii Dennis Flaherty. viii Myrleen Ferguson Cate/Photo Edit, Inc. ix R. Morley/PhotoLink/Photodisc Green/Getty Images. xi Chuck Place/Place Stock Photo. CA Standards (l) Nigel Cattlin/Photo researchers, Inc. (pc–tl) OSF/Fleetham, D./Animals Animals. (pc–tr) Frans Lanting/Minden Pictures. (pc–tcr) Tim Davis/Photo Researchers, Inc. (pc–bcr) Jane Burton/DK Images. (pc–br) M. Botzek/Zefa/Masterfile. (pc–bl) John Daniels/Ardea. (pc–bcl) Juniors Bildarchiv/Nature Company/Alamy. (pc–lc) Jane Burton/DK Images. (cl) Bios/Peter Arnold. (cr) Ernest A. Janes/Bruce Coleman. (tr) Jeff Foott/Bruce Coleman, Inc. (tcr) E. R. Degginger/Bruce Coleman, Inc. (bcr) Kevin R. Morris/Corbis. (br) Dominique Braud/Dembinsky Photo Associates, Inc. S1 Jose Luis Pelaez, Inc./Corbis. S3 Lonnie Duka/Index Stock Imagery. S4 Neal Mishler/GettyImages. S5 Mark A. Schneider/Visuals Unlimited. Unit A Opener: Martin Harvey/Wild Images. CA Field Trip (tr) Ralph A Clevenger/Corbis. (br) Michael Redmer/Visuals Unlimited. (bkgrd) Frans Laning/Corbis. v 1 J.C. Leacock/J.C. Leacock Photography. 2–3 Charles Mann/Photo Researchers. 4–5 Robert W. Ginn/Photo Edit, Inc. 5 (tr) Foodfolio/Alamy. (cl) Nicholas Eveleigh/Iconica/Getty Images. (cr) Chris Burrows/The Garden Picture Library. (bl) Aaron Haupt/Photo Researchers, Inc. 6 (t) Colin Keates/DK Images. (b) Richard Shiell. 6–7 (bkgrd) Art Wolfe. 10 (c), (br) © Dwight Kuhn. (bl) Philip Dowell/DK Images. 11 (cl) George D. Lepp/Corbis. (cr) Neil Fletcher & Matthew Ward/Dorling Kindersley/Getty Images. (b) Altrendo Nature/Getty Images. 14 Gibson Stock Photography. 18 (bl) Michael b. Gadomski/Photo Researchers, Inc. 20–21 Jonathan Blair/Getty Images.

21 (t) Royalty–Free/Corbis. 22 (bl) Gary Moon/Images in Natural Light. 22–23 (bkgrd) Dennis Flaherty. 23 Gary Moon/Images in Natural Light. 24 (bl) Stephen J. Krasemann/DRK Photo. 24–25 (bkgrd) Bill Ross/Corbis. 26 © Dwight Kuhn. 27 © E.R Degginger/Color–Pic, Inc. 28 (tl) Richard Shiell. 28–29 (b) Joseph G. Strauch, Jr. 29 (tr) Donald Specker/Animals Animals–Earth Scenes. 30–31 (bkgrd) Inga Spence/Visuals Unlimited. 31 Richard Shiell/Dembinsky Photo Associates. 32 (bl) N. Et Perennou/Photo Researchers, Inc. 32–33 (bkgrd) Chuck Place. 34 Dinodia Photo Library/Brand X Pictures/Alamy. 35 (tl) David Sieren/Visuals Unlimited. (tr) David Sieren/Visuals Unlimited. (cr) Michael Thompson/Earthscenes. 36 Dr. John Cunningham/Visuals Unlimited. 37 Joseph Devenney/The Image Bank/Getty Images. 39 (t) Photodisc/Getty Images. (b) Luiz C. Marigo/Alamy. 40 (tl) Philip Dowell/DK Images. 40 (tr) Gary Moon/Images in Natural Light. (bl) Richard Shiell. (br) Michael Thompson/Earthscenes. 42–43 (bkgrd) John Cancalosi/Nature Picture Library. 43 (tr) Elmar Krenkel/Zefa/Corbis. (cl) © Bill Horn/Acclaim Images. (cr) John Giustina/Taxi/Getty Images. (bl) IFA/eStock Photo/PictureQuest. 44–45 (bkgrd) Mitsuaki Iwago/Minden Pictures. 44 (t) © E.R. Degginger/Color–Pic, Inc. (c) Eric Lindgren/Ardea. (b) Kevin R. Morris/Corbis. 46–47 Nigel Cattlin/Photo Researchers, Inc. (pc–tl) OSF/Fleetham, D./Animals Animals. (pc–tr) Frans Lanting/Minden Pictures. (pc–tcr) Tim Davis/Photo Researchers, Inc. (pc–bcr) Jane Burton/DK Images. (pc–br) M. Botzek/Zefa/Corbis. (pc–bl) John Daniels/Ardea. (pc–bcl) Juniors Bildarchiv/Nature Company/Alamy. (pc–cl) Jane Burton/DK Images. (pc–tcl) Kevin Schafer/Corbis. 48 (bl) Bios/Peter Arnold. (br) Ernest A. Janes/Bruce Coleman. 49 (tr) Johnny Johnson/Drk Photo. (b) Jeff Foott/Bruce Coleman. 50 (tl) David R. Frazier/Photo Researchers, Inc. (tr) Don & Pat Valenti/DRK Photo. (bl), (br) © Dwight Kuhn 51 (tl) J.L. Lepore/Photo Researchers, Inc. (tr) Anthony Mercieca/Photo Researchers, Inc. (br) © Dwight Kuhn. (br) DK Images. 52 (bl) Gary Meszaros/Dembinsky Photo Associates. (br) Bob Jensen/Bruce Coleman Inc. 52–53 (bkgrd) Michael Hubrich/Dembinsky Photo Associates. 54 (bl) © E.R. Degginger/Color–Pic, Inc. (bc) E.R. Degginger/Bruce Coleman Inc. (br) Gary Meszaros/Bruce Coleman Inc. 54–55 (bkgrd) Marion Owen/AlaskaStock.com. 55 (bl) E.R. Degginger/Bruce Coleman Inc. (br) John Shaw/Bruce Coleman Inc. 56 © E.R. Degginger/Color–Pic, Inc. 56–57 (bkgrd) Garry Black/Masterfile. 57 © E.R. Degginger/ Color–Pic, Inc. 58 (bl) Tom Lazar/Earth Scenes/Animals Animals. 58–59 (bkgrd) Steve Maslowski/Visuals Unlimited, Inc. 60 John Daniels/Ardea. 61 Dick Luria/Taxi/Getty Images. 62 (tl) Joe McDonald/DRK Photo. (b) Kevin R. Morris/Corbis. 63 (tl) Jim Bourg/Reuters/Corbis. 66 (bl) Art Wolfe/Getty Images. 66–67 (bkgrd) Frans Lanting/Minden Pictures. 68–69 Ardea. 70 Dominique Braud/Dembinsky Photo Associates, Inc. 71 (tr) Carol Walker/naturepl.com. (cl) Don Mason/Corbis. (cr) Dominque Braud/Dembinsky Photo Associates, Inc. 72–73 (bkgrd) © Frank Siteman/Photo Edit, Inc. 75 (bkgrd) Courtesy of Dr. Ray Wack. 75 (tr) © Christopher Loviny/Corbis. 76 (t) Jeff Foott/Bruce Coleman. (tc) E.R. Degginger/

Bruce Coleman. (bc) Kevin R. Morris/Corbis. (b) Dominique Braud/Dembinsky Photo Associates, Inc. 80 (l) Ron Sanford/Corbis. (c) Ron Sanford/Corbis. (r) Claudia Adams/Dembinsky Photo Associates, Inc. Unit B Opener: Robert Harding World Imagery/Almay Images. CA Field Trip (tr) John Shaw/Bruce Coleman, Inc. (br) © John Cancalosi/DRK Photo. (bkgrd) Dennis Flaherty Photography. 81 © Art Wolfe, Inc. 82–83 © Ken Lucas/Visuals Unlimited. 84–85 (bkgrd) Tom Bean/DRK Photo. 85 (t) Steve Satushek/Getty Images. 85 (tc) © Fritz Poelking/The Image Works. (bc) © Royalty Free/Corbis. (b) © Mark A. Schneider/Visuals Unlimited. 86 (t) Tony Freeman/Photo Edit, Inc. (c) David Young–Wolff/Photo Edit, Inc. (b) Tom Bean/DRK Photo. 86–87 (bkgrd) Arthur M. Greene/Bruce Coleman Inc. 88 (bl) © Royalty Free/Corbis. 88–89 (bkgrd) © Bryan Dadswell/Alamy. 90 Mike Kipling Photography/Alamy Images. 91 Dietrich Leis Stock Photography. 92 (tl) © Vo Trung Dung/Corbis Sygma. (c) © E.R. Degginger/Color–Pic, Inc. (bl) Charles D. Winters/Photo Reasearchers, Inc. (br) DK Images. 93 (tr) Colin Keates/© DK Images Courtesey of the Natural history Museum, London. (cl) © Mark A. Schneider/Visuals Unlimited. (cr) Harry Taylor/Dorling Kindersley/Getty Images. (b) GC Minerals/Alamy Images. 94 (tl) Stephen J. Krasemann/DRK Photo. (cl) DK Images. (cr) Harry Taylor/DK Images. (b) © E.R. Degginger/Dembinsky Photo Associates, Inc. 95 (t) Andreas Einsiedel/DK Images. (bl) © E.R. Degginger/Color Pic, Inc. (bc) Mark A. Schneider/Photo Researchers, Inc. 95 (br) Harry Taylor/DK Images. 96–97 (bkgrd) © Susan E. Degginger/Color–Pic, Inc. 98 J. David Andrews/Masterfile. 99 (tl) © E.R. Degginger/Color–Pic, Inc. (tr) Rod Planck/Photo Researchers, Inc. (b) Tom Bean/DRK Photo. 100 Stephen J. Krasemann/DRK Photo. 101 (tl) Brian Miller/Bruce Coleman Inc. (c) Thomas Dressler/DRK Photo. (b) © Wally Eberhart/Visuals Unlimited. 102–103 (bkgrd) © Royalty Free/Corbis. 106 © Richard Cummins/Corbis. 107 (t) David Young–Wolff/Photo Edit, Inc. (bc) John William Banagan/The Image Bank/Getty Images. (br) © E.R. Degginger/Color–Pic, Inc. 108 (l) Holt Studios/Nigel Cattlin/Photo Researchers, Inc. (r) © Dwight Kuhn/Bruce Coleman Inc. 109 George D. Lepp/Corbis. 112 (bl) Francois Gohier/Photo Researchers, Inc. 112–113 Kazimieras Mizgiris/AFIAP/Mizgiris Amber Museum. 115 (tr) Alvis Upitis/Superstock. (cr) William P. Leonard/DRK Photo. (br) William P. Leonard/DRK Photo. 116–117 DK Images. 117 (t) Bob Jensen/Bruce Coleman, Inc. (r) Frank Staub/Index Stock Imagery. 118 (bl) Ed Reschke/Peter Arnold, Inc. (br) Charles R. Belinky/Photo Researchers, Inc. 119 (tc) Francois Gohier/Photo Researchers, Inc. (tr) Tom Bean/DRK Photo. (br) T.A. Wiewandt/DRK Photo. 120 © NHPA/Daniel Heuclin. 120–121 (bkgrd) © William Leonard/DRK Photo. 121 (t) © Soqui Ted/Corbis Sygma. 122 © Alber J. Copley/Visuals Unlimited. 123 © Paul A. Souders/Corbis. 124 (tl) Andreas Einsiedel/DK Images. (tr–inset) © Richard Cummins/Corbis. (bl), (br) Tom Bean/DRK Photo. 126–127 (bkgrd) Craig C. Sheumaker/

Credits